Table of Contents

About Author

Vishal Garg is a software engineer with a passion for designing applications. He has passion for learning new technologies and share the knowledge with everyone. He is a developer who is expert in technologies like Angular, Knockout Js, .Net core, C# etc. Most of his time is spent on building Angular applications but he also shares his knowledge with the community through book writings, blog writings , presentations etc.

About Book

Angular Simplified is designed to help developers learn the basic concepts of Angular and how to build an web application using Angular. I have shared lot of practical examples in this book , so that user can emulate them and get better understanding on each topic of Angular. This book provides the fundamental knowledge on Angular concepts. I have kept this book as simple and as concise as possible so that user can learn about fundamental concepts of Angular without wasting any amount of time. I hope you will find the material of this book helpful and looking forward to publish more versions in future.

1. Introduction

1.1 What is Angular ?

- Angular is a JavaScript framework written in typescript.
- Single page applications (SPA) are build using Angular
- Web, desktop and mobile applications are build by using Angular

1.2 Why Angular?

1. Automatic Synchronization :-

Angular provides **Two-way binding** using which data is automatically synchronized between model(typescript component) and view (html template).

2. Reusability :-

The **component** based architecture of Angular makes the code reusable across whole application.

3.Ease of unit testing :-

Since we have **independent components**, unit testing is much easier in angular applications.

4.Modular Structure :-

Modules make angular application easy to maintain and also provides benefits of lazy loading i.e. to load the features on-demand

5.Typescript :-

Angular application is built in Typescript (a superset of JavaScript). Typescript provides more features in terms of type checking, early error catching, debugging etc.

6.Efficient :-

Angular provides highly optimized bundle sizes. It has smaller file sizes and hence faster component loading.

7.Ease of Maintenance :-

Decoupled components are easy to maintain i.e. they can be easily replaced, removed or added. This makes updates in application easy.

1.3 Project Setup

To setup an Angular application you need following :-

1.Node.js :-

First install node.js to your local machine. We need **npm**(node package manager) in Angular applications to manage dependencies and libraries .

Installation path:- https://nodejs.org/en/download/

Here, you can select version and platform

2.IDE :-

you need a IDE to run Angular application. There are many IDE's available in market to run angular applications. Some are listed below :-

- Visual Studio Code
- Visual Studio
- Webstorm
- Sublime text

3.CLI :-

The CLI (command line interface) approach is highly recommended to setup a Angular project because it's easy and provides optimized code.

Open your terminal or command prompt and write following command :-

```
npm install -g @angular/cli
```

4.Create the Workspace :-

Now, navigate to the location where you want to create your Angular project and run the following command :-

```
ng new my-app
```

new :- Create a new Project (Installs necessary packages and files of project)

my-app:- Name of your Project

5.Run the Application :-

Navigate to your project folder and run the following commands :-

```
cd my-app
```

```
ng serve --open
```

ng serve :- builds the application

--open(optional) :- Automatically opens the application in browser

<u>**1.4 CLI Commands**</u>

Commands	Result
Ng new <Project name>	Create New Project
Ng serve	Test the application
Ng serve --o	Build and run the application
Ng build	Compile the application
Ng build --prod	Create Dist folder to deploy code to production environment
Ng deploy <Project name>	Deploy the application
Ng **g c** <Component name>	**G**enerate the **C**omponent in application with .spec and .css files
Ng **g c** --skipTests=true --s <Component name>	**G**enerate **C**omponent without .spec and .css files
Ng **g s** <Service name>	**G**enerate **S**ervice
Ng **g s** --skiptests=true <Service name>	**G**enerate **S**ervice without .spec file
Ng **g cl** <Model name> --type=model	**G**enerate Model **cl**ass
Ng add <Library name>	Add 3rd part libraries e.g.:- @angular/material
Ng update	To update project packages and libraries
Ng lint	Check quality of code

<u>Angular CLI Schematics</u>

To add or update something in project

1. **ng generate** :- Generate components, services, routes using CLI commands
2. **ng add** :- Add third party libraries in a project
3. **ng update** :- update package or libraries in project

<u>Angular builders</u>

1. **ng build** :- compile the application
2. **ng lint** :- check quality of code
3. **ng deploy** :- deploy the application

<u>**1.5 Project Structure**</u>

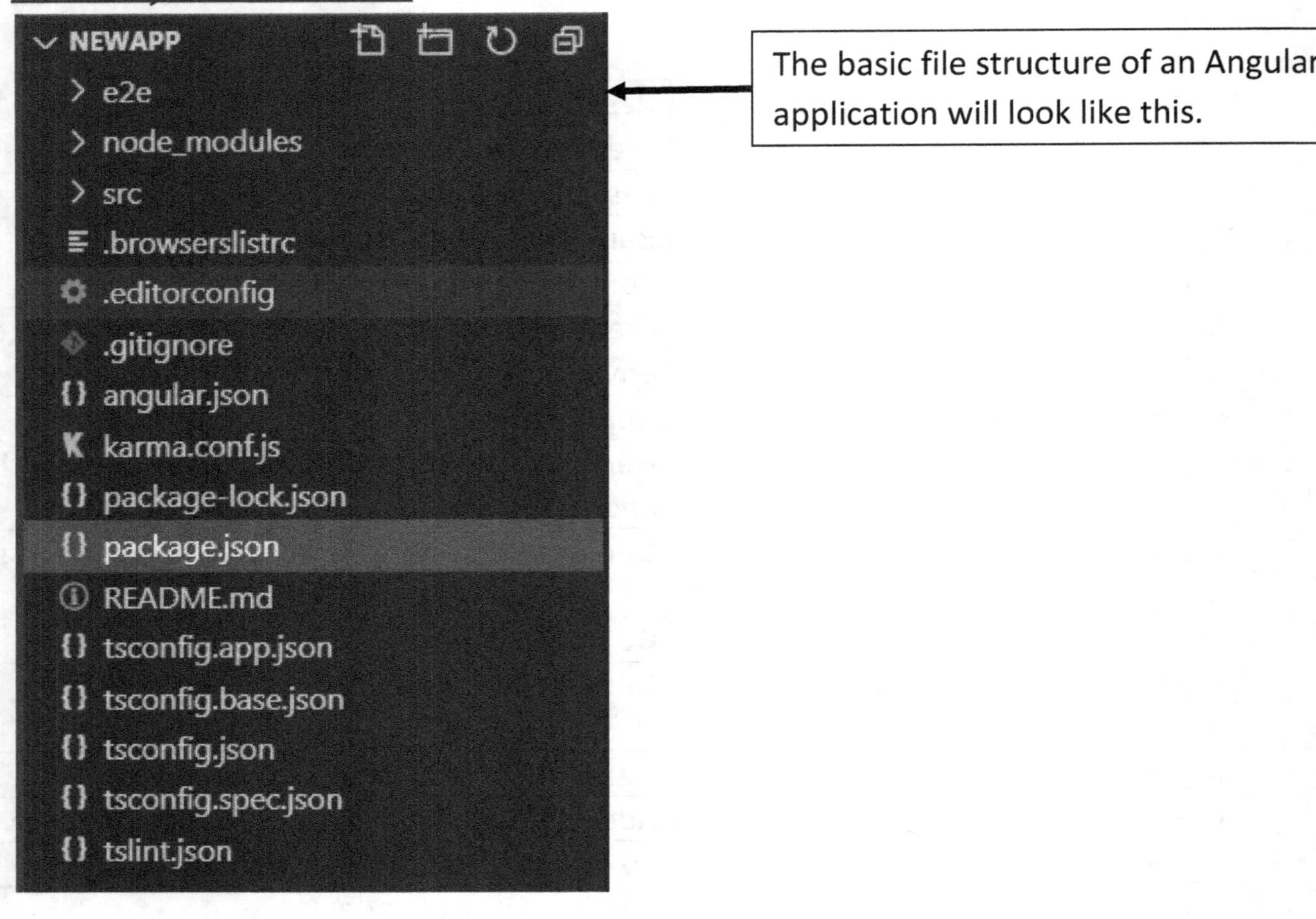

The basic file structure of an Angular application will look like this.

package.json

package.json is a json file which holds the metadata information and manages projects' dependencies , version, script etc.

Dependencies packages in package.json are :-

- **Angular packages** - Angular core packages(@angular/)
- **3rd party packages** - 3rd party libraries required in application
- **polyfill packages** - polyfills emulates features which are missing in some browsers

CLI command to add 3rd party library

tsconfig.json

It contains instructions to convert or transpile typescript file(.ts) to JavaScript file(.js). The tsconfig.json file contains the root files and the compiler options required to compile the project

tsconfig.base.json :- Contains information on the compiler

```
/* To learn more about this file see: https://angular.io/config/tsconf
ig. */
{
  "compileOnSave": false,
  "compilerOptions": {
    "baseUrl": "./",
    "outDir": "./dist/out-tsc",
    "sourceMap": true,
    "declaration": false,
    "downlevelIteration": true,
    "experimentalDecorators": true,
    "moduleResolution": "node",
    "importHelpers": true,
    "target": "es2015",
    "module": "es2020",
    "lib": [
      "es2018",
      "dom"
    ]
  }
}
```

tsconfig.app.json :- Contains configuration information for the application

```
/* To learn more about this file see: https://angular.io/config/tsconf
ig. */
{
  "extends": "./tsconfig.base.json",
  "compilerOptions": {
    "outDir": "./out-tsc/app",
    "types": []
  },
  "files": [
    "src/main.ts",
    "src/polyfills.ts"
  ],
  "include": [
    "src/**/*.d.ts"
  ]
}
```

tsconfig.spec.json :- Contains typescript configuration for the **Tests** in application
Like, **Jasmine** is used for testing.

```
/* To learn more about this file see: https://angular.io/config/tsconf
ig. */
{
  "extends": "./tsconfig.base.json",
  "compilerOptions": {
    "outDir": "./out-tsc/spec",
    "types": [
      "jasmine"
    ]
  },
  "files": [
    "src/test.ts",
    "src/polyfills.ts"
  ],
  "include": [
    "src/**/*.spec.ts",
    "src/**/*.d.ts"
  ]
}
```

<u>**tslint.json**</u> **:-** Contains the linting configuration for the application. Linting is a tool to flag errors, style errors, best practices errors, bugs etc.

<u>**angular.json**</u> :- Contains project specific configuration. It defines structure of application and includes project settings.

Some of the settings are :-

- **Environment** :- Environment settings like (development, production) is specified here

```
"configurations": {
  "production": {
    "fileReplacements": [
      {
        "replace": "src/environments/environment.ts",
        "with": "src/environments/environment.prod.ts"
      }
    ],
```

- **Styles and Scripts :-** Styles and scripts settings are also added here. Bootstrap files are also added here

```
"styles": [
  "src/styles.css"
],
"scripts": []
},
```

- **Root files** :- Root files settings are also included here

```
"outputPath": "dist/NewApp",
"index": "src/index.html",
"main": "src/main.ts",
"polyfills": "src/polyfills.ts",
"tsConfig": "tsconfig.app.json",
```

- **Compiler :-** Complier settings are also included here. Like we can set AOT complier true or false from here

```
"aot": true,
```

- **Resources :-** Resource settings like any icons, images or assets are also included here

```
"assets": [
    "src/favicon.ico",
    "src/assets"
],
```

- **Test :-** Test settings are included here

```
"test": {
  "builder": "@angular-devkit/build-angular:karma",
  "options": {
    "main": "src/test.ts",
    "polyfills": "src/polyfills.ts",
    "tsConfig": "tsconfig.spec.json",
    "karmaConfig": "karma.conf.js",
    "assets": [
      "src/favicon.ico",
      "src/assets"
    ],
    "styles": [
      "src/styles.css"
    ],
    "scripts": []
  }
},
```

- **Lint :-** Lint settings are included here

```
"lint": {
  "builder": "@angular-devkit/build-angular:tslint",
  "options": {
    "tsConfig": [
      "tsconfig.app.json",
      "tsconfig.spec.json",
      "e2e/tsconfig.json"
    ],
    "exclude": [
      "**/node_modules/**"
    ]
  }
},
```

- **Project information** :- It contains version, schematic etc. information

```
"$schema": "./node_modules/@angular/cli/lib/config/schema.json",
"version": 1,
"newProjectRoot": "projects",
"projects": {
  "NewApp": {
    "projectType": "application",
    "schematics": {},
    "root": "",
    "sourceRoot": "src",
    "prefix": "app",
```

Karma.conf.js :- It contains the testing tools required for the project, the environment for testing and any specific action which may be required for testing purpose.

```javascript
module.exports = function (config) {
  config.set({
    basePath: '',
    frameworks: ['jasmine', '@angular-devkit/build-angular'],
    plugins: [
      require('karma-jasmine'),
      require('karma-chrome-launcher'),
      require('karma-jasmine-html-reporter'),
      require('karma-coverage-istanbul-reporter'),
      require('@angular-devkit/build-angular/plugins/karma')
    ],
    client: {
      clearContext: false // leave Jasmine Spec Runner output visible in browser
    },
    coverageIstanbulReporter: {
      dir: require('path').join(__dirname, './coverage/NewApp'),
      reports: ['html', 'lcovonly', 'text-summary'],
      fixWebpackSourcePaths: true
    },
    reporters: ['progress', 'kjhtml'],
    port: 9876,
    colors: true,
    logLevel: config.LOG_INFO,
    autoWatch: true,
    browsers: ['Chrome'],
    singleRun: false,
    restartOnFileChange: true
  });
};
```

node_modules :- This folder contains the libraries downloaded from npm. This folder should not be deployed as it automatically download packages from package.json

src folder :- This folder contains the main code files like components (.ts), modules, templates(.html), stylesheets(.css), environment configuration etc.

Let's see the functionalities of each file or folder present in **src** folder

main.ts :-

- The code in the main.ts file gets executed first
- Main.ts creates a browser environment for application
- This file bootstraps(starts) the whole application by passing App module from app.module.ts

```typescript
import { enableProdMode } from '@angular/core';
import { platformBrowserDynamic } from '@angular/platform-browser-dynamic';

import { AppModule } from './app/app.module';
import { environment } from './environments/environment';

if (environment.production) {
  enableProdMode();
}

platformBrowserDynamic().bootstrapModule(AppModule)
  .catch(err => console.error(err));
```

bootstraps(starts) the app by loading appModule

index.html :-

This is the entry file which contains the root level component of whole application

```html
<!doctype html>
<html lang="en">
<head>
  <meta charset="utf-8">
  <title>NewApp</title>
  <base href="/">
  <meta name="viewport" content="width=device-width, initial-scale=1">
  <link rel="icon" type="image/x-icon" href="favicon.ico">
</head>
<body>
  <app-root></app-root>
</body>
</html>
```

Root level component

<u>**polyfills.ts:-**</u>

This file contains code that is used to provide **compatibility support** for older browsers. polyfills fills the missing features of browsers that do not support latest versions of JavaScript specifications.

<u>**styles.css:-**</u>
Global CSS file for whole Angular application.

<u>**test.ts:-**</u>
It is a **main test file** used by Angular CLI command (ng test) to execute all unit tests in a application.

<u>**assets folder :-**</u>

This folder contains the resource files like images, icons, locales etc. which are used in application.

<u>**app folder :-**</u>

This folder contains the component, modules files which you have created for your Angular application.

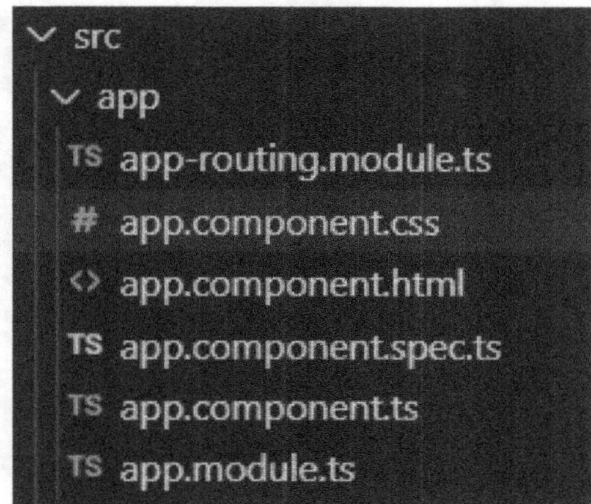

<u>**app-routing.module.ts :-**</u>

This module file contains **routing configuration** and it is loaded from root module i.e. app.module.ts. Though routing configuration can be placed in root module (app.module.ts) as well but it is best practice to place routing configuration in separate module file.

```typescript
import { NgModule } from '@angular/core';
import { Routes, RouterModule } from '@angular/router';

const routes: Routes = [];

@NgModule({
  imports: [RouterModule.forRoot(routes)],
  exports: [RouterModule]
})
export class AppRoutingModule { }
```

app.component.css :-

This file contains **CSS styles** for app component

app.component.html :-

This file contains the **view** of component. It is a template which is used corresponding to a component (typescript file).

app.component.spec.ts :-

This file is a **unit testing** file corresponding to a app component. It is executed by Angular CLI command (ng test).

app.component.ts :-

This is a **component** file written in typescript which contains the logic of component.

```typescript
import { Component } from '@angular/core';

@Component({
  selector: 'app-root',
  templateUrl: './app.component.html',
  styleUrls: ['./app.component.css']
})
export class AppComponent {
  title = 'NewApp';
}
```

app.module.ts :-

This is a **main module** file written in typescript which includes all the
dependencies of a application. All the modules, components, root component are
registered here.

```typescript
import { BrowserModule } from '@angular/platform-browser';
import { NgModule } from '@angular/core';

import { AppRoutingModule } from './app-routing.module';
import { AppComponent } from './app.component';

@NgModule({
  declarations: [
    AppComponent
  ],
  imports: [
    BrowserModule,
    AppRoutingModule
  ],
  providers: [],
  bootstrap: [AppComponent]
})
export class AppModule { }
```

2. Flow

Lets understand the flow of Angular application. Like how files are executed in sequential order.

1. Angular.json

Angular.json Contains all configurations of Angular application. Builder look into this file for all the paths and configurations to load main file(main.ts)

```
"options": {
        "outputPath": "dist/NewApp",
        "index": "src/index.html",
        "main": "src/main.ts",
```

2. Main.ts

Main.ts is a entry point of the application. It calls the function bootstrapModule(AppModule)

```
import { enableProdMode } from '@angular/core';
import { platformBrowserDynamic } from '@angular/platform-browser-dynamic';

import { AppModule } from './app/app.module';
import { environment } from './environments/environment';

if (environment.production) {
  enableProdMode();
}

platformBrowserDynamic().bootstrapModule(AppModule)
  .catch(err => console.error(err));
```

3.App.module.ts

App.module.ts:- In main.ts we are bootstrapping AppModule. AppModule is defined in App.module.ts. It is a main module file which is bootstrapping root component

```typescript
import { BrowserModule } from '@angular/platform-browser';
import { NgModule } from '@angular/core';

import { AppRoutingModule } from './app-routing.module';
import { AppComponent } from './app.component';

@NgModule({
  declarations: [
    AppComponent
  ],
  imports: [
    BrowserModule,
    AppRoutingModule
  ],
  providers: [],
  bootstrap: [AppComponent]
})
export class AppModule { }
```

4.App.component.ts

App.component.ts:- In app.module.ts we are bootstrapping Appcomponent(App.component.ts). This is a main component file which contains the logic (.ts file) and template(.html file)

```typescript
import { Component } from '@angular/core';

@Component({
  selector: 'app-root',
  templateUrl: './app.component.html',
  styleUrls: ['./app.component.css']
})
export class AppComponent {
  title = 'NewApp';
}
```

5.Index.html

Index.html :- Angular app is aware of all the modules, components, styles, scripts of the application at this point. Now, index.html is executed which contains root component app-root

```html
<!doctype html>
<html lang="en">
<head>
  <meta charset="utf-8">
<title>NewApp</title>
<base href="/">
<meta name="viewport" content="width=device-width, initial-scale=1">
<link rel="icon" type="image/x-icon" href="favicon.ico">
</head>
<body>
  <app-root></app-root>
</body>
</html>
```

6.App.component.html

App.component.html :- This file contains all the html elements. Contents of this file are displayed at the start of a application.

3. Architecture of Angular

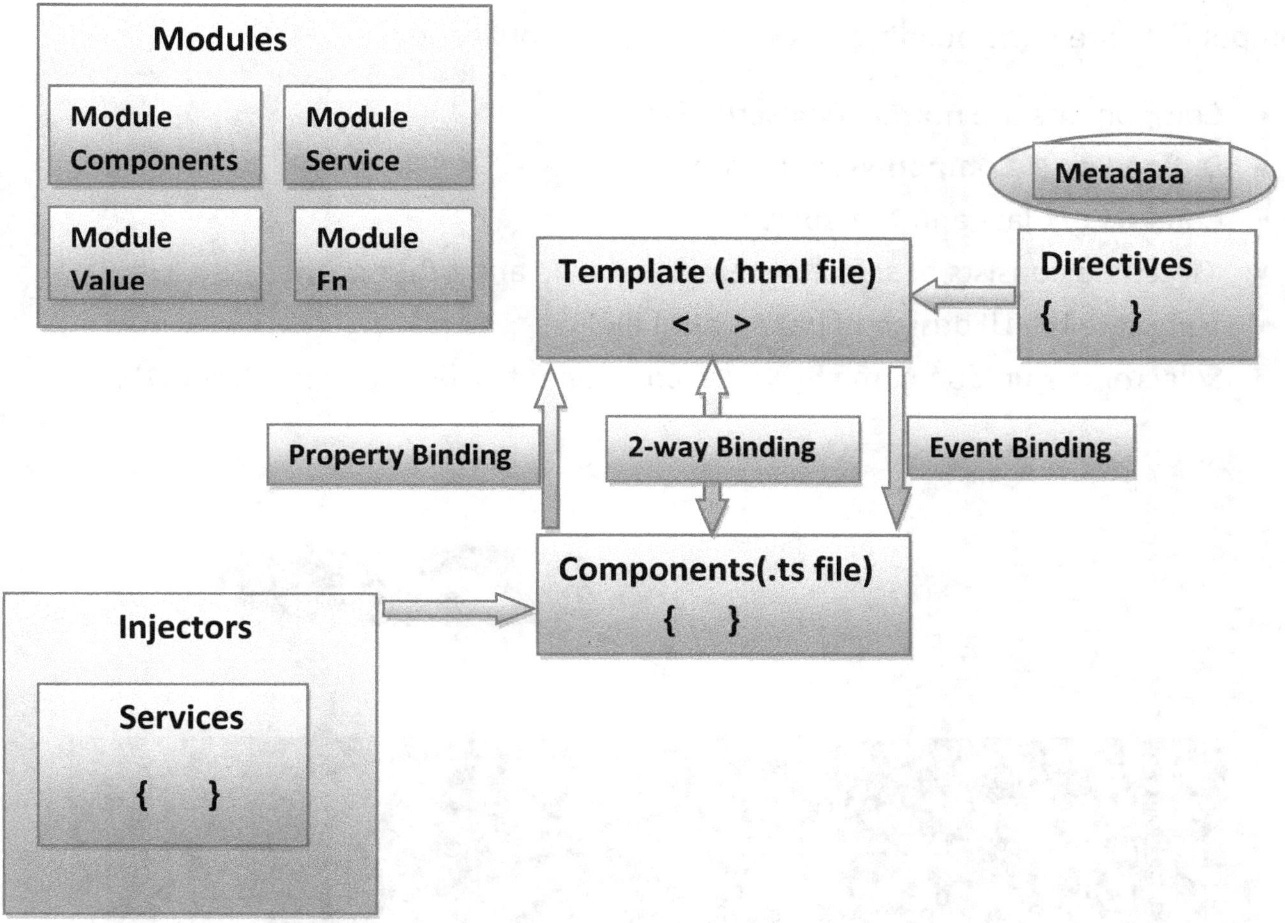

Key components of an Angular app are:-

1. Components
2. Modules
3. Data Binding
4. Directives
5. Templates
6. Metadata
7. Services and Dependency Injection

4. Components

Components are basic building blocks in a angular application

- Components are normal typescript class
- Defined by **@Component** decorator
- Consists of Class and Metadata
- Metadata consists of selector, template, style and other properties
- Template is a UI design of page (.html file)
- Selector is a unique name by which component is identified in Html DOM

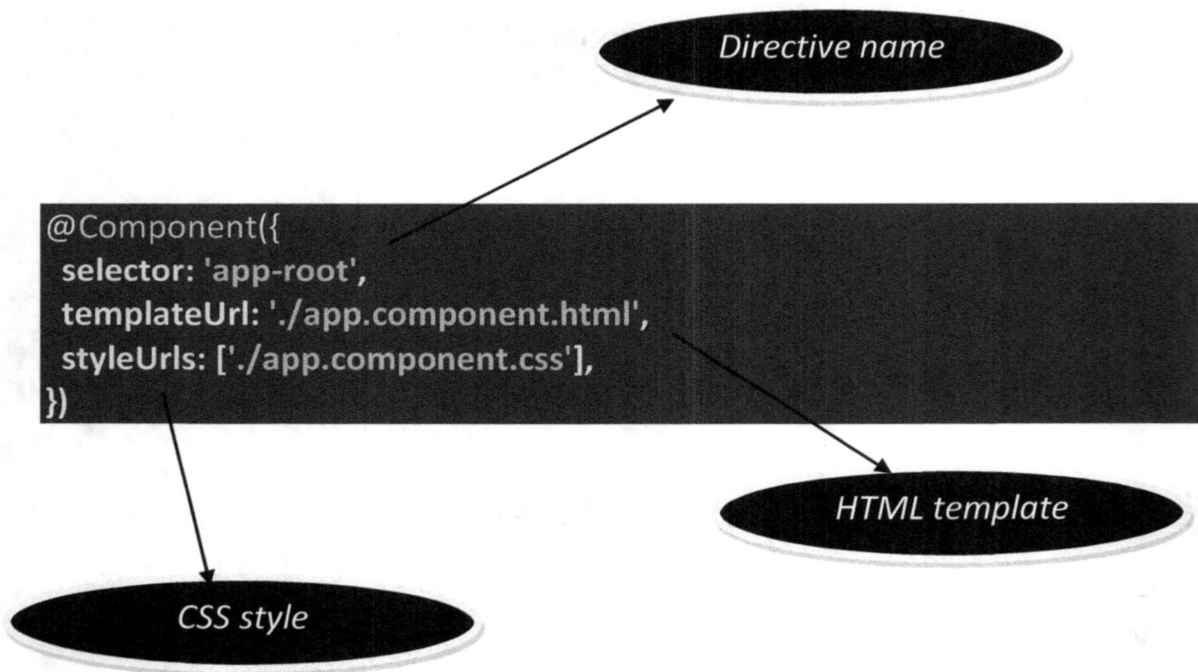

5. Modules

- Module is a bundling of building blocks like components, directives, pipes, routes, services.
- **@NgModule** decorator is used to create a module class
- One root module is always required in angular application
- Module can be split into multiple modules like we can have routing module which handles routing feature only and this module is then included in root module
- Every component of a application needs to be registered in a module

NgModule has 4 properties:-

1. **declarations : register every component here**
2. **imports :   import every module here**
3. **providers: provide services used in app**
4. **bootstrap: root component of app**

e.g.

app.module.ts

```typescript
import { BrowserModule } from '@angular/platform-browser';
import { NgModule } from '@angular/core';
import { AppComponent } from './app.component';
import { LoginComponent } from './login/login.component';
import { LoginService } from './shared/login.service';
import { AppRoutingModule } from './app-routing.module';
import { HttpClientModule } from '@angular/common/http';

@NgModule({
  declarations: [
    AppComponent,
    LoginComponent
```

declarations array :- Here we need to register all our components that we are using in application.

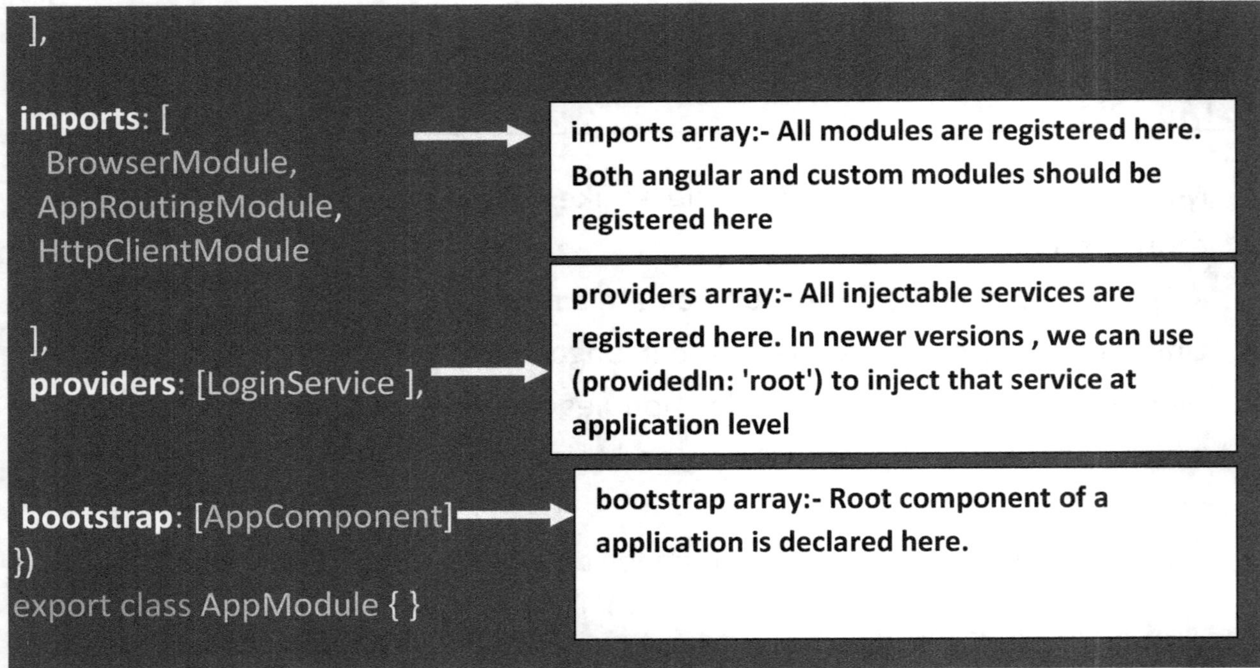

Every module is a standalone module i.e. you need to export the module to root module in order to use that module at application level.

e.g. :- We can create separate routing module , but we still need to export this routing module to our root module(app module)

<u>app-routing.module.ts</u>

```typescript
import { LoginComponent } from './login/login.component';
import { NgModule } from '@angular/core';
import { Routes, RouterModule } from '@angular/router';

const routes: Routes = [
    { path: 'login', component: LoginComponent},
    { path: '', component: LoginComponent},
];

@NgModule({
  imports: [RouterModule.forRoot(routes)],
  exports: [RouterModule]
})
export class AppRoutingModule { }
```

6. Data Bindings

Data binding is a process of establishing a connection between user interface template (Html file) and its component(typescript file)

Using Data binding typescript code (business logic) communicates with its template (user interface)

Data binding = Communication

Types of Data Bindings:-

1. **String Interpolation**

2. **Property Binding**

3. **Event Binding**

4. **Two-Way Binding**

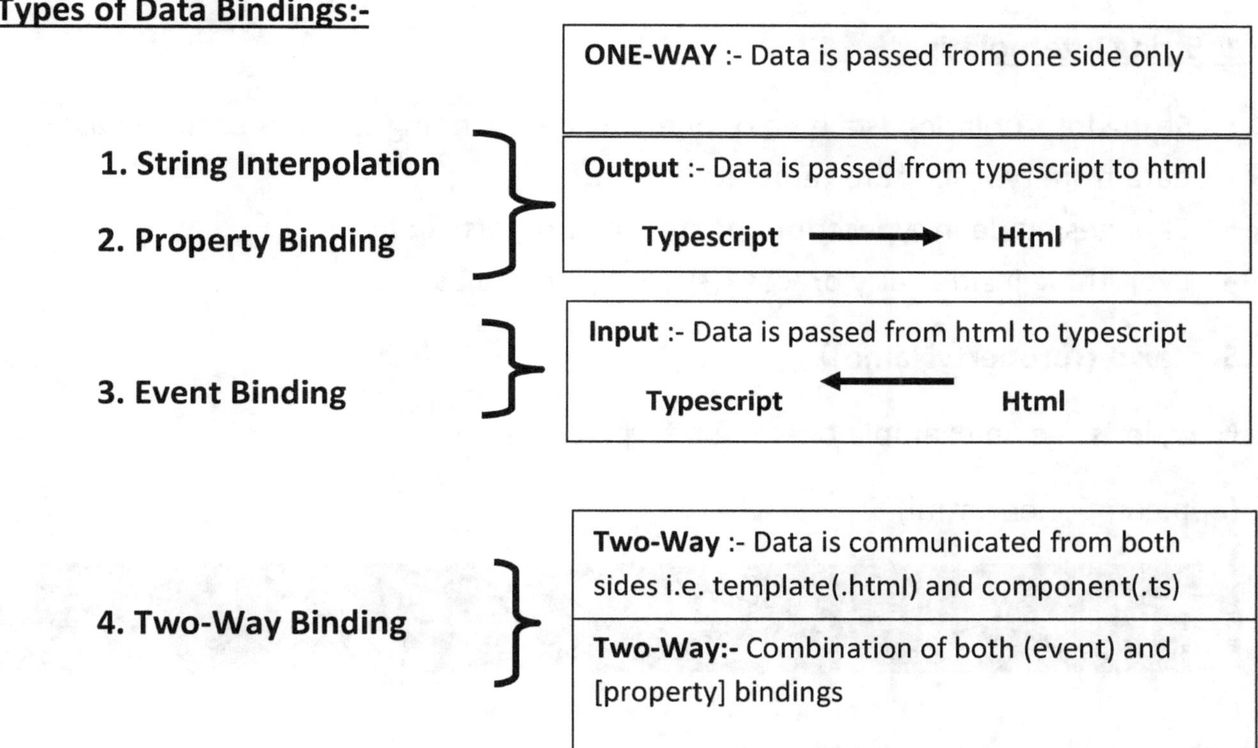

One-Way Binding (Output) -

- **OUTPUT** data from typescript code to html code in template

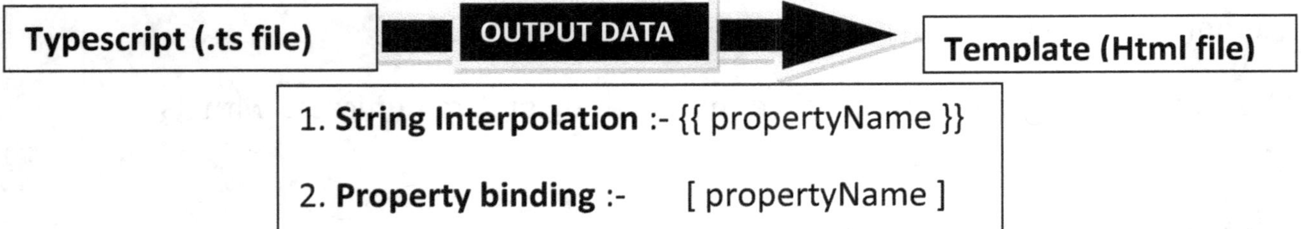

1. String Interpolation

- String Interpolation is a type of one-way data binding which is used to pass data from typescript to template (html).
- Changes made in typescript updates the property in html
- Everything inside curly braces {{}} is interpreted as a string

Syntax :- {{propertyName}}

Now, let's see an example of string interpolation

(app.component.html)

```html
<div>
   <p>Default title is : {{ title}} </p>
</div>
```

(app.component.ts)

```typescript
import { Component } from '@angular/core';

@Component({
   selector: 'app-root',
   templateUrl: './app.component.html',
   styleUrls: ['./app.component.css']
})
export class AppComponent {
   title = 'String Interpolation';
```

1-way communication - Data is passed from typescript to html template. Value of 'title' property will be reflected in html view.

```
}
```

(output)

Default title is : String Interpolation

2. Property Binding

- Property Binding is a type of one-way data binding which is used to dynamically bind DOM properties of html elements.
- Changes made in typescript updates the property in html

Syntax :- [propertyName]

Now, let's see an example of property binding

(app.component.html)

```
<div>
  <p><input type="text" [value]= title [disabled]=isTrue></p>
</div>
```

(app.component.ts)

```
import { Component } from '@angular/core';

@Component({
  selector: 'app-root',
  templateUrl: './app.component.html',
  styleUrls: ['./app.component.css']
})
export class AppComponent {
  title = 'Property binding';
  isTrue = true;
}
```

1- way communication - data is passed from typescript to template. We are binding the [disabled]property of html element to 'isTrue' which is coming from typescript

(output)

One-Way Binding (Input) -

- Data is passed from template to typescript

3. Event Binding

- Event Binding capture events raised in template (html file) and a event handler in component (typescript class) will handle these events
- Data from events is passed from template to typescript
- **$event** can be passed as argument in (event) to access event data

Syntax :- (eventName)

Now, let's see an example of event binding

(app.component.html)

```
<div>
  <p><input type="text" [value]= title [disabled]=isTrue></p>
</div>
<div>
  <button (click)="onChange()">Change title</button>
</div>
```

(app.component.ts)

```
import { Component } from '@angular/core';
@Component({
  selector: 'app-root',
  templateUrl: './app.component.html',
  styleUrls: ['./app.component.css'],
})
export class AppComponent {
  title = 'one way binding';
  isTrue = true;
```

Event binding - In this case event is raised from html file and we have event handler in typescript file. So, data is flowing from view to component.

```
onChange(): void {
   this.title = 'event binding';
}
}
```

(output)

(before button is clicked)

one way binding

Change title

(After button is clicked)

event binding

Change title

4. Two-Way Binding

- In Two way data binding data is communicated from component(typescript) to view(html) and vice- versa.
- It's a combination of both (event) and [property] binding
  (event) + [property] = [(Two way binding)]
- **ngModel** directive is used for two-way data binding
- **FormsModule** library needs to be imported in App.module.ts as ngModel is not a part of angular library

Syntax :- [(ngModel)]

Let's see an example for two way data binding

For two-way binding(ngModel) we need to import FormsModule

(app.module.ts)

```
import { BrowserModule } from '@angular/platform-browser';
```

```typescript
import { NgModule } from '@angular/core';

import { AppRoutingModule } from './app-routing.module';
import { AppComponent } from './app.component';
import { FormsModule } from '@angular/forms';

@NgModule({
  declarations: [AppComponent],
  imports: [BrowserModule, AppRoutingModule, FormsModule],
  providers: [],
  bootstrap: [AppComponent],
})
export class AppModule {}
```

(app.component.html)

```html
<div>
  <p><input type="text" [value]= title  [(ngModel)]="title"></p>
</div>
<p>
  <label>New title is : </label>
  <input type="text" [value]= title>
</p>
```

(app.component.ts)

```typescript
import { Component } from '@angular/core';

@Component({
  selector: 'app-root',
  templateUrl: './app.component.html',
  styleUrls: ['./app.component.css'],
})
export class AppComponent {
  title = 'two way binding';
}
```

(output)

default values -

two way binding

New title is : two way binding

When user changes value in first text box, it gets reflected in second text box as well because of two way data binding

new value

New title is : new value

Pass data between Components (@Input() and @Output())

A parent component cannot access the properties of child component because in angular the scope of property is limited to its component only. Even parent component cannot access the properties of child component

To share data between parent and child components, we can use 2 properties provided by angular -

- **@input()**
- **@output()**

7. @Input()

- @Input() property is used to pass data from Parent component to child component

- Use **@Input() decorator** with a property in **child component** in order to receive data from parent component
- Import **Input** from '**@angular/core**' library

Syntax:- @Input() propertyName;

Let's see an example of @input

(child.component.ts - child component)

```typescript
import { Component, Input } from '@angular/core';

@Component({
  selector: 'app-child',
  templateUrl: './child.component.html',
  styles: [],
})
export class ChildComponent {
  constructor() {}
  @Input() childProperty = 'default child component';
}
```

Added @Input() decorator with childProperty so that this property can be accessed from its parent

(child.component.html)

```html
<div style="border: 1px solid;"><h4>child component</h4>
<input type="text" [value]= childProperty>
</div>
```

(app.component.ts - parent component)

```typescript
import { Component } from '@angular/core';

@Component({
  selector: 'app-root',
  templateUrl: './app.component.html',
  styleUrls: ['./app.component.css'],
})
export class AppComponent {
  title = 'Input property';
}
```

(app.component.html)

```html
<div style="border: 1px solid">
  <h4>parent component</h4>
  <p><input type="text" [value]="title" [(ngModel)]="title" /></p>

  <p>
    <app-child [childProperty]="title"></app-child>
  </p>
</div>
```

<app-child> is a child component directive

[childProperty] - It's a property of child component which is accessible here because of @Input() decorator in child component.

(output)

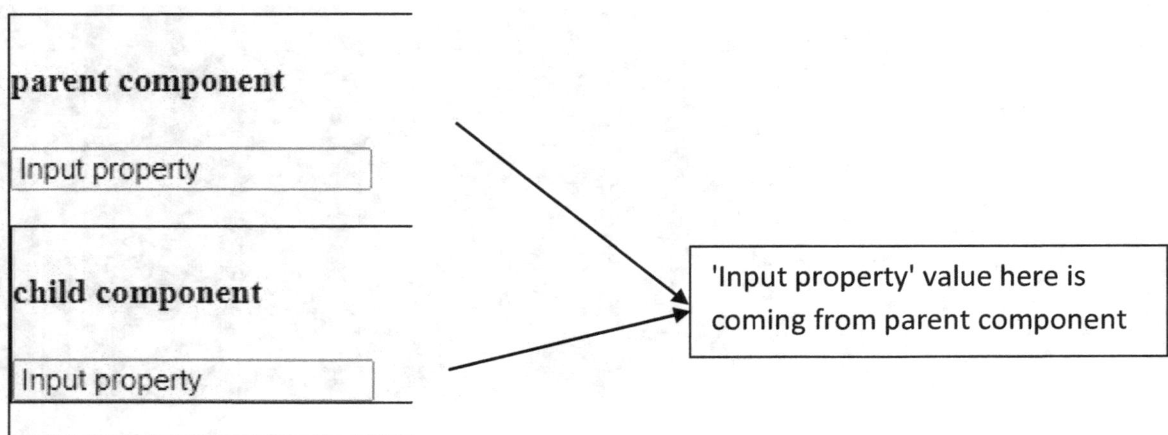

Aliasing

We can also assign alias name to the property using @input()

Syntax:- @Input('aliasName') propertyName;

8. @Output()

- @Output() property is used to pass data from child component to parent component

- Create a custom event in child component to emit values to its parent component
- **EventEmitter** is used to create a custom events
- Use **@Output() decorator** with a event property in **child component** in order to emit data to parent component
- Import **output** from '**@angular/core**' library
- Import **EventEmitter** from '**@angular/core**' library

Syntax:- @Output() eventName = new EventEmitter<T>();

Let's see an example of @OutPut()

First, let's add a custom event emitter in child component

(child.component.ts - Child Component)

```typescript
import { Component, EventEmitter, Output } from '@angular/core';

@Component({
  selector: 'app-child-output',
  templateUrl: './child-output.component.html',
  styleUrls: ['./child-output.component.css'],
})
export class ChildOutputComponent {
  constructor() {}
  textValue = 'default';
  @Output() childProperty = new EventEmitter<string>();

  AddToParent(item: string): void {
    this.childProperty.emit(item);
  }
}
```

@Output() - make childProperty event accessible from parent component

emit value from childProperty

EventEmitter :- Create a custom event to emit values from child to parent component

(child.component.html)

```html
<div style="border: 1px solid">
  <h4>child component</h4>
  <input type="text" [value]="textValue" [(ngModel)]="textValue" />
</div>
<div>
  <button (click)="AddToParent(textValue)">Add to Parent</button>
</div>
```

(app.component.html)

```html
<div style="border: 1px solid">
  <h4>parent component</h4>
  <p><input type="text" [value]="title" [(ngModel)]="title" /></p>

  <p>
    <app-child (childProperty)="GetValue($event)"></app-child>
  </p>
</div>
```


(app.component.ts)

```typescript
import { Component } from '@angular/core';

@Component({
  selector: 'app-root',
  templateUrl: './app.component.html',
  styleUrls: ['./app.component.css'],
})
export class AppComponent {
  title = 'Input property';
  GetValue(event: string) {
    this.title = event;
  }
}
```

(output)

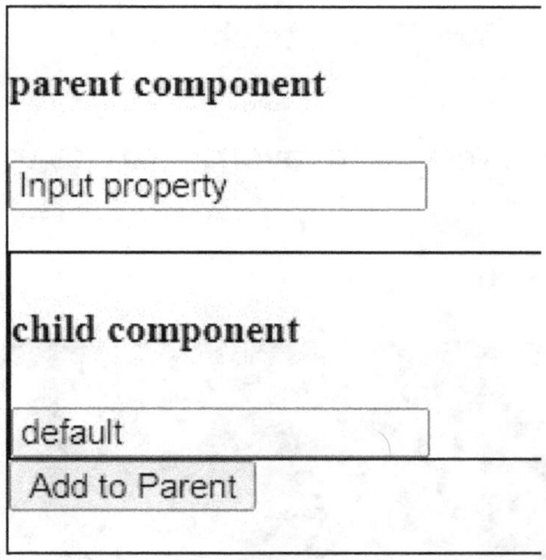

parent component

Input property

child component

default
Add to Parent

After clicking 'Add to Parent', value from child component will be added to parent component

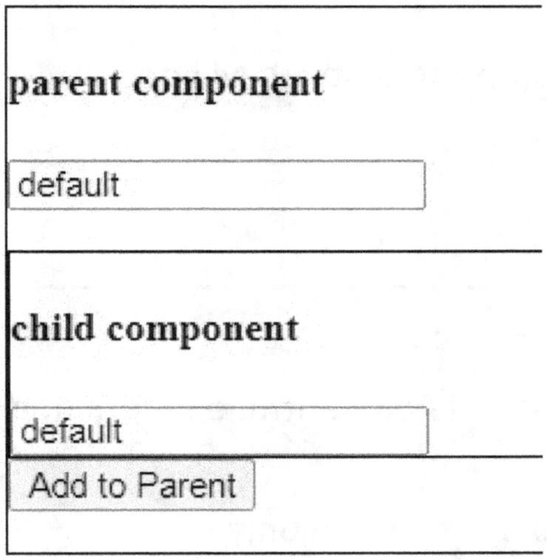

parent component

default

child component

default
Add to Parent

Aliasing

We can also assign alias name to the property using @Output()

Syntax:- @Output('aliasName') propertyName;

<u>**Passing Styles from Parent to child component (ViewEncapsulation)**</u>

9. ViewEncapsulation

- Styles applied to particular component are not overridden to child components
- Add **Encapsulation** property in @Component directive to override styles to child components
- Import **ViewEncapsulation** from '@angular/core' library

```
@Component({
selector: 'app-root',
templateUrl: './app.component.html',
styleUrls: ['./app.component.css'],
encapsulation: ViewEncapsulation.None
})
```

ViewEncapsulation.None :- It will apply all parent component styles to child

VIewEncapsulation.Emulated(Default) :- Parent component styles will not override styles of child component.

10. Local reference in template

- Local reference variable will hold the reference of whole html element and all its properties
- Scope of local reference variable is limited to its template only

Syntax:- #variableName

Let's see an example

(app.component.html)

```html
<div id="pd" style="border: 1px solid">
  <h4>parent component</h4>

  <p><input type="text" [value]="title" #name /></p>
  <p>
    <app-child-output (childProperty)="GetValue(name)"></app-child-
output>
  </p>
  <p>Local ref. value is : {{ title }}</p>
</div>
```

Local reference variable

(app.component.ts)

```typescript
import { Component } from '@angular/core';

@Component({
  selector: 'app-root',
  templateUrl: './app.component.html',
  styleUrls: ['./app.component.css']
  })
export class AppComponent {
  title = 'Input property';

  GetValue(element: HTMLInputElement) {
    this.title = element.value;
  }
}
```

Html Input element is accessed and its value is assigned to title

(output)

parent component

Test !!

child component

default
Add to Parent

Local ref. value is : Test !!

Value of input text box using local reference variable

11. ViewChild

- Html DOM elements can be accessed in typescript file by using ViewChild decorator
- Local reference variable or component name can be passed as argument in ViewChild
- Import **ViewChild** from '@angular/core'

Syntax: @ViewChild(reference selector, { static: true }) variableName: ElementRef;

Let's see an example of ViewChild

(app.component.ts)

```
import { Component, ElementRef, ViewChild } from '@angular/core';

@Component({
  selector: 'app-root',
  templateUrl: './app.component.html',
  styleUrls: ['./app.component.css'],
})
```

```typescript
export class AppComponent {
  title = 'Input property';
  @ViewChild('name', { static: true }) name: ElementRef;

  GetValue() {
    this.title = this.name.nativeElement.value;
  }
}
```

(app.component.html)

```html
<div id="pd" style="border: 1px solid">
  <h4>parent component</h4>
  <p><input type="text" [value]="title" #name /></p>
  <p>
    <app-child-output (childProperty)="GetValue()"></app-child-output>
  </p>
  <p>Local ref. value is : {{title}}</p>
</div>
```

(output)

parent component

viewchild test

child component

default

Add to Parent

Local ref. value is : viewchild test

Value of input element is accessed in typescript using **ViewChild**

12. ng-content

- ng-content is used to place content inside component's opening and closing tag
- By default, any content inside component will be lost
- ng-content acts as placeholder to project content into components

Syntax: <ng-content>

Let's see an example of ng-content

(app.comonent.html - parent component)

```html
<div id="pd" style="border: 1px solid">
  <h4>parent component</h4>
  <p>
    <app-child(childProperty)="GetValue()">Test data here</app-child>
  </p>
</div>
```


(child.component.html - child component)

```html
<div style="border: 1px solid">
  <h4>child component</h4>
  <ng-content></ng-content>
</div>
```

(output)

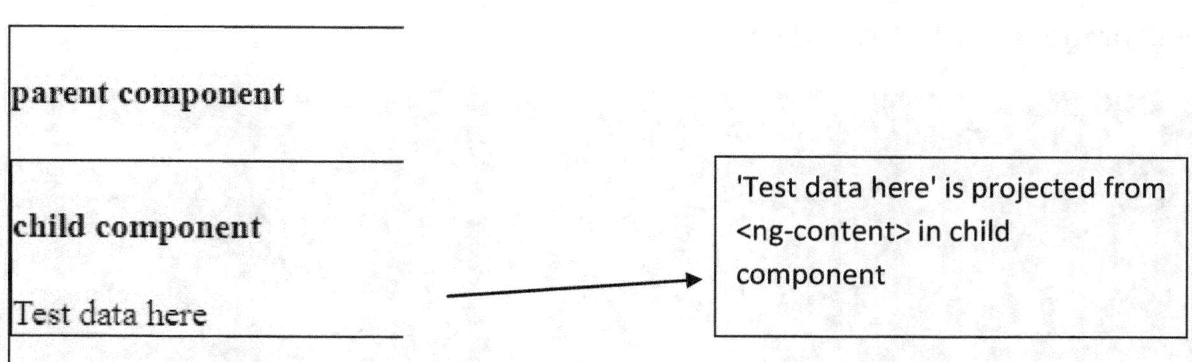

13. ContentChild

- Element or component inside <ng-content> can be accessed in typescript file by using ContentChild decorator
- Local reference variable or component name can be passed as argument in ContentChild
- Import **ContentChild** from '@angular/core'

Syntax: @ContentChild(reference selector, { static: true }) variableName: ElementRef;

Let's see an example of ContentChild

(app.component.html - parent component)

```html
<div id="pd" style="border: 1px solid">
  <h4>parent component</h4>
  <p>
    <app-child (childProperty)="GetValue()">
    <p #varName>
      Test data here
    </p>
    </app-child>
  </p>
</div>
```

(child.component.html - child component)

```html
<div style="border: 1px solid">
  <h4>child component</h4>
  <ng-content></ng-content>
</div>

<div>
  <button (click)="AddToParent(textValue)">Add to Parent</button>
</div>
```

(child.component.ts - child component)

```typescript
import {
  Component,
  ContentChild,
  ElementRef,
  EventEmitter,
  Output,
} from '@angular/core';

@Component({
  selector: 'app-child',
  templateUrl: './child-output.component.html',
  styleUrls: ['./child-output.component.css'],
})
export class ChildOutputComponent {
  constructor() {}
  textValue = 'default';

  @Output() childProperty = new EventEmitter<string>();
  @ContentChild('varName', { static: true }) varName: ElementRef;

  AddToParent(item: string): void {
  this.childProperty.emit(item);

   console.log('content child value: ' +
   this.varName.nativeElement.textContent);
  }
}
```

(output)

parent component

child component

Test data here

| Add to Parent |

```
Angular is running in development mode.
[WDS] Live Reloading enabled.
content child value:  Test data here
>  |
```

In console log, you can see that 'test data here' is printed with the help of **ContentChild**

<u>**14. Lifecycle Hooks**</u>

- Lifecycle hooks are events which gets triggered at specific points of component's life
- There are 8 stages in a life cycle of a component
- These 8 life cycle hooks gets triggered in a sequential order

8 life cycle hooks in sequential order in which they are triggered are :-

1. **ngOnChanges**
2. **ngOnInit**
3. **ngDoCheck**
4. **ngAfterContentInit**
5. **ngAfterContentChecked**
6. **ngAfterViewInit**
7. **ngAfterViewChecked**
8. **ngOnDestroy**

Order of Execution

1. ngOnChanges

- Called every time a data-bound **Input Property** changes
- It is the **first hook** to be called in a lifecycle
- It's the only hook which receives an argument. It receives a **SimpleChanges** object which contains previous and current values of a input property
- **OnChanges** interface should be implemented
- import **OnChanges** and **SimpleChanges** from **'@angular/core'** library

Example -
(child.component.ts)

```typescript
import { OnChanges, SimpleChanges } from '@angular/core';
import { Component, Input, OnInit } from '@angular/core';

@Component({
  selector: 'app-child',
  templateUrl: './child.component.html',
  styles: [],
})
export class ChildComponent implements OnInit, OnChanges {
  @Input() childElement: string;
  constructor() {
    console.log('constructor called');
  }
  ngOnChanges(changes: SimpleChanges): void {
    console.log('ngOnChanges called : ' + changes);
  }
  ngOnInit(): void {
    console.log('ngOnInit called');
  }
}
```

(child.component.html)

```html
<div>
  <p>Child Component</p>
  <p><input type="text" [value]="childElement"></p>
</div>
```

(app.component.ts)

```typescript
import { Component } from '@angular/core';

@Component({
  selector: 'app-root',
  templateUrl: './app.component.html',
  styleUrls: ['./app.component.css'],
```

```
})
export class AppComponent {
  title = 'LifeCycle';

  Change(name: string): void {
    this.title = name;
  }
}
```

(app.component.html)

```
<div>
  <p>Parent Component</p>
  <input type="text" [value]="title" #name>
  <p><button (click)="Change(name.value)">Change</button></p>
  <p><app-child [childElement]="title"></app-child></p>
</div>
```

(output)

First time page is loaded :-

Parent Component

LifeCycle

Change

Child Component

LifeCycle

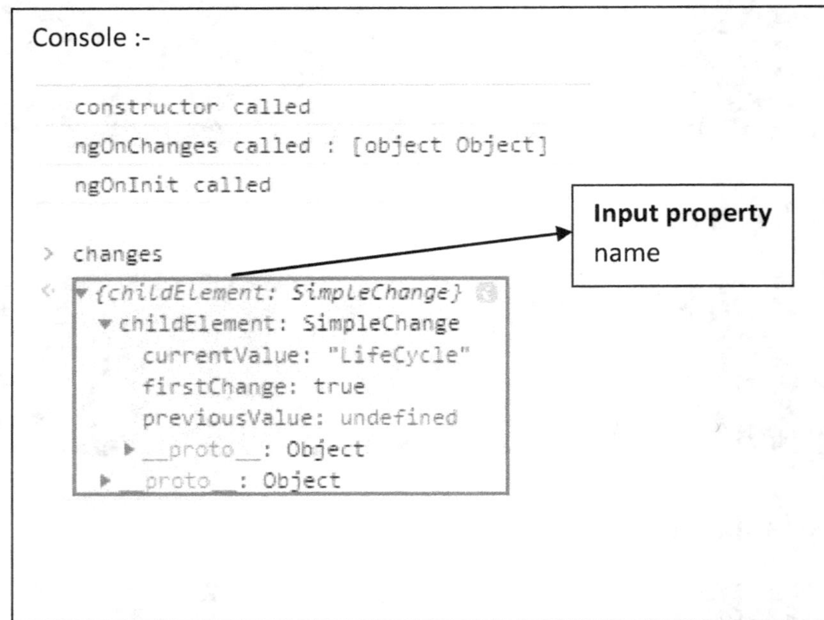

Now, If we do any change and click the 'change' button then :-

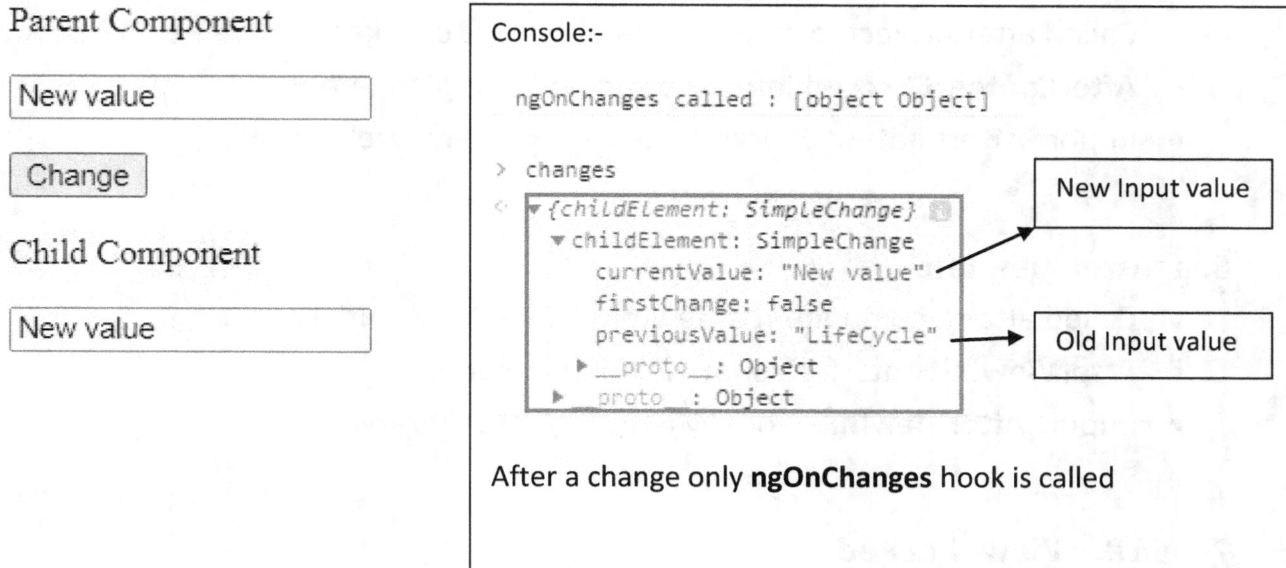

2. ngOnInit

- Called on initialization of a component
- It is the called **after** the **Constructor**.
- **OnInit** interface should be implemented
- import **OnInit** from **'@angular/core'** library

3. ngDoCheck

- Called at every change detection cycle
- Use this hook instead of **ngOnChanges** as it may conflict if both hooks are used together
- **DoCheck** interface should be implemented
- import **DoCheck** from **'@angular/core'** library

4. ngAfterContentInit

- Called after content(ng-content) is projected in the component
- **AfterContentInit** interface should be implemented

- import **AfterContentInit** from **'@angular/core'** library

5. ngAfterContentChecked

- Called after projected content(ng-content) is checked
- **AfterContentChecked** interface should be implemented
- import **AfterContentChecked** from **'@angular/core'** library

6. ngAfterViewInit

- Called after a component's view(or child view) is initialized
- **AfterViewInit** interface should be implemented
- import **AfterViewInit** from **'@angular/core'** library

7. ngAfterViewChecked

- Called after a component's view(or child view) is checked
- **AfterViewChecked** interface should be implemented
- import **AfterViewChecked** from **'@angular/core'** library

8. ngOnDestroy

- Called once a component is about to get destroyed
- Mainly used for cleanup and unsubscribe purposes
- **OnDestroy** interface should be implemented
- import **OnDestroy** from **'@angular/core'** library

15. Directives

- Directives are instructions which gets executed whenever compiler finds it in DOM
- There are 3 types of directives
    1. **Component Directive** -
        - Directives with templates.
        - These directives have their own custom HTML attached with them
    2. **Structural Directive** -
        - DOM layout is changed i.e. an element is added or not to a DOM structure
        - Structural directives are prefixed with asterisk(*) symbol.
        - e.g. ***ngIf** and ***ngfor** are structural directives
    3. **Attribute Directive** -
        - Appearance or behavior of an element, component etc. is changed
        - e.g. **ngStyle**

1. Component Directive -

These are custom directives i.e. in this directive a custom template is attached corresponding to a component.

Let's see a basic example of component directive -

In this example, we have created new component by the name of "directive.component.ts"

(directive.component.ts)

```
import { Component, OnInit } from '@angular/core';

@Component({
  selector: 'app-directive',
  templateUrl: './directive.component.html',
  styles: [],
})
export class DirectiveComponent implements OnInit {
  constructor() {}
```

```
  ngOnInit(): void {}
}
```

(directive.component.html)

```
<p>directive works!</p>
```

Now, we are using this directive (app-directive) in the html DOM of other component

(app.component.html)

```
<p>Hello App component !!</p>
<app-directive></app-directive>
```

> It acts as a placeholder. business logic and template from component (directive.component.ts) is replaced here

(output) -

Hello App component !!

directive works!

> Html of directive.component.html is added to the DOM of app.component.html

2. Structural Directive

These are pre-defined directives which manipulates the html DOM.
Structural Directive changes the DOM structure i.e. it adds or removes html elements from DOM structure

Some commonly used Structural directives are -

- ***ngIf**
- ***ngFor**
- **ngSwitch**

***ngIf -**

It's a conditional statement i.e. show or hide some html elements based on a condition.

Let's see an example -

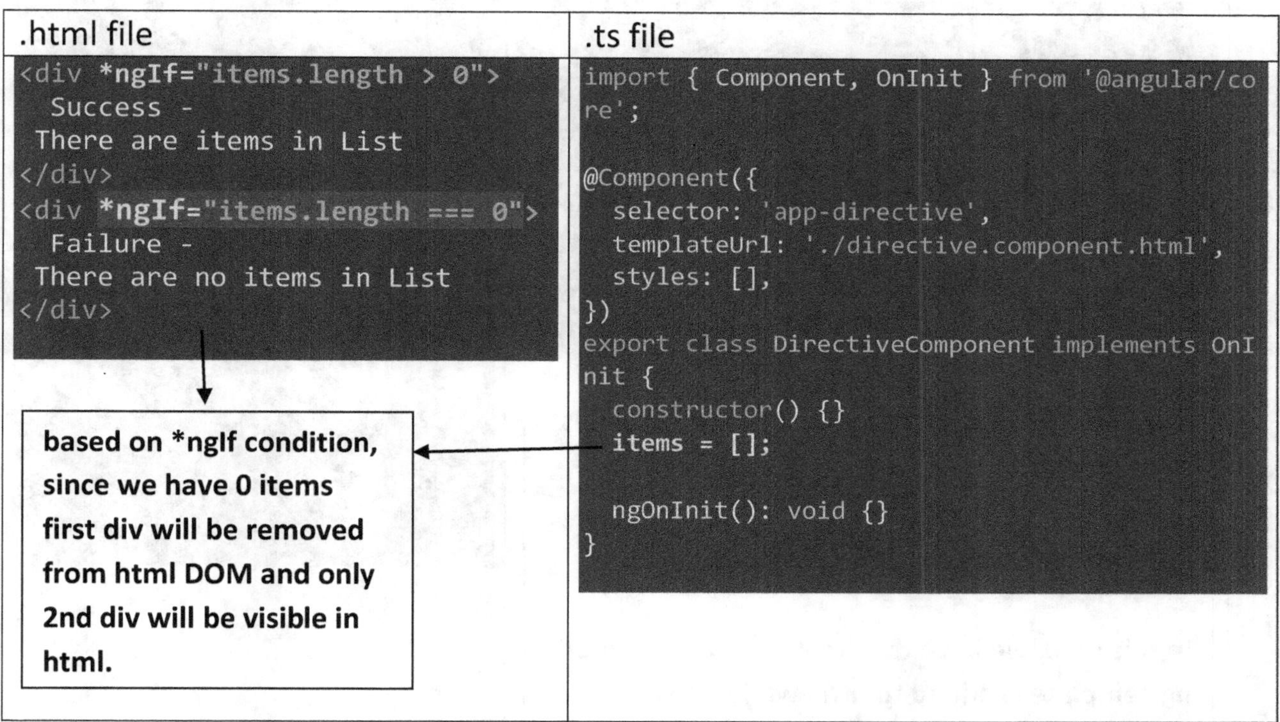

.html file	.ts file

``html
<div *ngIf="items.length > 0">
  Success -
  There are items in List
</div>
<div *ngIf="items.length === 0">
  Failure -
  There are no items in List
</div>
``
 	
based on *ngIf condition, since we have 0 items first div will be removed from html DOM and only 2nd div will be visible in html.
	``typescript
	import { Component, OnInit } from '@angular/core';
	
	@Component({
	  selector: 'app-directive',
	  templateUrl: './directive.component.html',
	  styles: [],
	})
	export class DirectiveComponent implements OnInit {
	  constructor() {}
	  items = [];
	
	  ngOnInit(): void {}
	}
	``

(output) -

Hello App component !!

Failure - There are no items in List

<u>***ngIf with else -**</u>

We can also add else with *ngIf to show or hide html elements based on conditions. But to use else condition we need ng-template directive

<u>**ng-template -**</u>

It acts as a placeholder for if else conditions.

Let's see an example with else condition

<table>
<tr><td>

.html file

```
<div *ngIf="items.length > 0 ; then suc
cess else failure">
</div>
<ng-template #success>
  Success - There are items in List
</ng-template>
<ng-template #failure>
  Failure - There are no items in List
</ng-template>
```

#success or #failure are local referencing names of ng-template.

We show or hide these ng-template blocks based on ngIF else condition

In this case, we have data in items array so first ng-template is added to html while 2nd ng-template is removed from html DOM

</td><td>

.ts file

```
import { Component, OnInit } from
'@angular/core';

@Component({
  selector: 'app-directive',
  templateUrl:
  './directive.component.html',
  styles: [],
})
export class DirectiveComponent
implements OnInit {
  constructor() {}
  items = [1, 2];

  ngOnInit(): void {}
}
```

</td></tr>
</table>

(output) -

Hello App component !!

Success - There are items in List

*ngFor -

Used for iterating list of objects

Let's see an example to iterate list of elements -

<table>
<tr><td>.html file</td><td>.ts file</td></tr>
<tr><td>

```html
<div *ngIf="items.length > 0 ; then su
ccess else failure">
</div>
<ng-template #success>
  Success - There are items in List
<ul>
<li *ngFor="let item of items">{{item}
}
</li>
</ul>
</ng-template>
<ng-template #failure>
  Failure - There are no items in List
</ng-template>
```

</td><td>

```typescript
import { Component, OnInit } fro
m '@angular/core';

@Component({
  selector: 'app-directive',
  templateUrl:
  './directive.component.html',
  styles: [],
})
export class DirectiveComponent
implements OnInit {
  constructor() {}
  items = [1, 2];

  ngOnInit(): void {}
}
```

</td></tr>
</table>

using *ngFor we are iterating over list of items and printing every single item one by one

ngSwitch -

- Show or hide one element from list of elements based on a condition.
- ngSwitch uses property binding instead of asterisk(*)
- ngSwitch is a structural directive consists of 2 more structural directives -
  ***ngSwitchCase** and ***ngSwitchDefault**

Let's see an example of ngSwitch

.html	.ts
| ```html
<div [ngSwitch]="color">
<div *ngSwitchCase="'RED'">Color is Red
<div *ngSwitchCase="'BLUE'">Color is Blue
<div *ngSwitchDefault>Default Color is Black

``` | ```ts
import { Component, OnInit } from '@angular/core';

@Component({
  selector: 'app-switch',
  templateUrl: './switch.component.html',
  styles: [],
})
export class SwitchComponent implements OnInit {
  constructor() {}
  color = 'RED';
  ngOnInit(): void {}
}
``` |

We have applied ngSwitch attribute on a color variable which is defined as 'RED' in its corresponding typescript file.

(output) -

Hello App component !!

Color is Red

***ngSwitchCase** is a structural directive because it adds or removes a html element based on a condition

***ngSwitchDefault** is also a structural directive because in this case a default value is added to html DOM in case no switch condition is satisfied

3. Attribute Directive -

These directives changes behavior or properties of an element.

Attribute directive do not change the DOM structure, It only adds or removes properties of a Html element.

Some commonly used Attribute directives are -

- **ngStyle**
- **ngClass**

ngStyle -

ngStyle is a attribute directive which dynamically updates the style of html elements

Let's see an example of ngStyle

```
<div>
  <label for="">Enter Color: </label>
  <input type="text" [(ngModel)]="color">
  <div [ngStyle]="{backgroundColor: color}">Color is {{color}}</div>
</div>
```


(output) -

Hello App component !!

Enter Color: red
Color is red

Hello App component !!

Enter Color: [green]
Color is green

ngClass -

ngClass is a attribute directive which dynamically adds or removes CSS classes based on a condition.

Let's see an example of ngClass

(.css file)

```css
.myColor{
   background-color: red;
}
```


(.html file)

```html
<div>
  <label for="">Enter Color: </label>
  <input type="text" [(ngModel)]="color">
  <div [ngClass]="{myColor: color==='red'}">Color is {{color}}</div>
</div>
```


(output) -

Hello App component !!

Enter Color: [red]
Color is red

Now, if you check this Div element in Developer tools of browser you can verify
that "myColor" class is added if the color is "red"

```
<div _ngcontent-sug-c45 ng-reflect-ng-class="[object Object]" class="myColor">
Color is red</div> == $0
```

Now, if we input any other color apart from 'red' the myColor class will not be
added to div element because condition is not satisfied in this case

Hello App component !!

Enter Color: blue

Color is blue

```
<div _ngcontent-sug-c45 ng-reflect-ng-class="[object Object]" class>Color is blue
</div>
```

In this case, 'myColor' class is not added since condition is not satisfied.

16. Pipes

- Pipes transform your output

```
{{ value | uppercase }}
```

Pipe :- this will transform output to uppercase letters

- Parameters can be passed in pipes using colon(:)

```
{{ value | date : 'fullDate' | uppercase }}
```

- Multiple parameters can be passed using multiple colons (:)
- Custom pipes can be created using **@pipe** decorator
- Computed values in Pipes do not get updated by default. You can add **'Pure'** property to get updated values

Custom Pipe

- Pipe and PipeTransform libraries need to be imported
- Add **@pipe** decorator
- Override the **transform** method which is implemented from **PipeTransform**

```typescript
import { Pipe, PipeTransform } from '@angular/core';

@Pipe({
  name: 'filter',
  pure: false
})
export class FilterPipe implements PipeTransform {

  transform(value: any, filterString: string, propName: string): any {
    // .... custom pipe
  }
}
```

17. Services with Dependency Injection

- Services can be any reusable typescript class
- We need not create instance of service to use it, instead we be using dependency injector provided by Angular

Dependency Injector

- Injects dependency (instance of service class) into component
- **Constructors** are used to inject services into components
- Add **providers** property in your component where you want to use service
- **providers** property can be added in **AppModule** to provide application level scope for a service

```
import { BrowserModule } from '@angular/platform-browser';
import { NgModule } from '@angular/core';
import { AppComponent } from './app.component';
import { UserService } from './user/service';


@NgModule({
declarations: [
AppComponent
  ],
  imports: [
   BrowserModule
  ],
  providers: [UserService],
  bootstrap: [AppComponent]
})
export class AppModule { }
```

<u>**Hierarchical injector**</u>

- Scope of service flows from top to bottom i.e. from highest level (AppModule) to component level
- Service instance in child component will override same instance from parent component

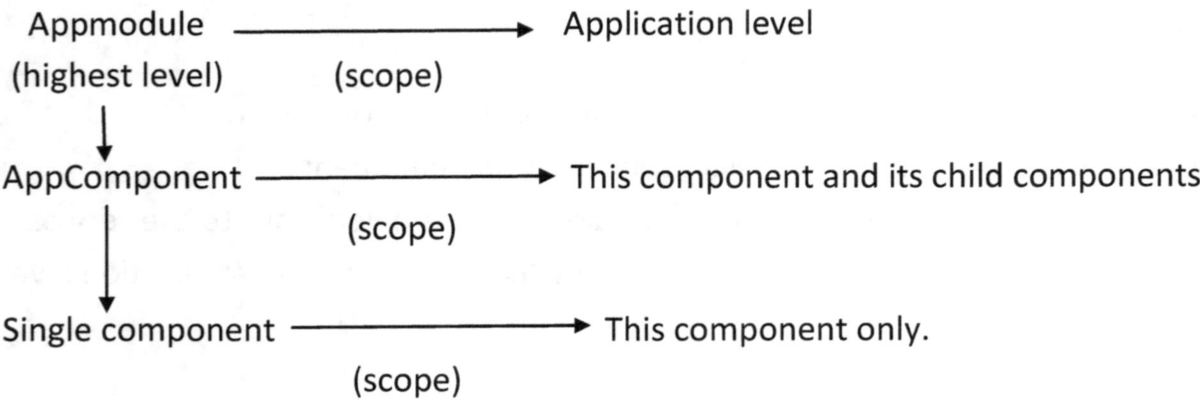

<u>**Nested Services**</u>

- One service can be injected into other services
- **@Injectable** decorator needs to be added to a receiving service class, where you need to inject another service to it.

Note:-

In new Angular versions, new approach is introduced to provide service in your application .

Instead of using providers array in Appmodule, you can now use

@Injectable({providedIn: 'root'}) in service components to provide application-wide scope.

e.g.:-

```
import { HttpClient } from '@angular/common/http';
import { Injectable } from '@angular/core';
import { Observable } from 'rxjs';

@Injectable({
  providedIn: 'root',
})
export class LoginService {
  constructor(private http: HttpClient) {}

  ServiceMethod1() { .... }
  ServiceMethod2() { .... }
}
```

18. Forms

Forms in Angular are used to handle user's input. It is used for data entry forms like login, register pages etc.

2 approaches for building forms in Angular

1. Template-driven
2. Reactive

Template-driven	Reactive
Form objects are created in Html **DOM**	Form objects are created programmatically in **typescript** file and synchronized with Html DOM elements
Easy Scenarios	Complex Scenarios
Two way data **binding** using **ngModel**	**Immutable** i.e. no data binding since typescript file already have access to form objects
Complex form **validations** are **cumbersome**	Complex form **validations** are **easy** to implement
Imported using **FormsModule**	Imported using **ReactiveFormsModule**
Not easy to test	Easy to test

1. Template-driven form

In template-driven forms we write logic, validations, controls etc. in the template part of the code (html file). It uses 2-way binding using ngModel.

//Html file(.html)

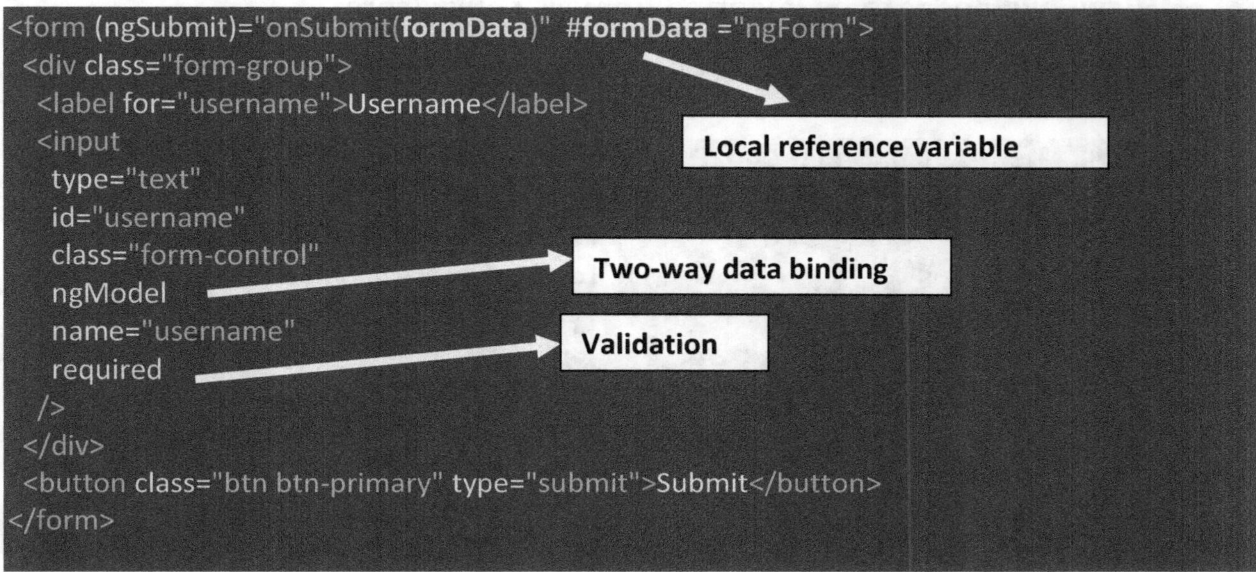

```html
<form (ngSubmit)="onSubmit(formData)" #formData ="ngForm">
 <div class="form-group">
  <label for="username">Username</label>
  <input
   type="text"
   id="username"
   class="form-control"
   ngModel
   name="username"
   required
  />
 </div>
 <button class="btn btn-primary" type="submit">Submit</button>
</form>
```


//Typescript file(.ts)

```typescript
import { Component} from '@angular/core';
import { NgForm } from '@angular/forms';

@Component({
 selector: 'app-root',
 templateUrl: './app.component.html',
 styleUrls: ['./app.component.css']
})
export class AppComponent {

  onSubmit(formData: NgForm) {
  console.log('submitted form values : ' + formData);
 }
}
```

<u>**1.1 Submitting form using ViewChild**</u>

- **@ViewChild** can be used to avoid passing of local form variable from html form to submit event in typescript file
- **ViewChild** needs to be imported from @angular/core

//Html file

```html
<form (ngSubmit)="onSubmit()"  #formData ="ngForm">
 <div class="form-group">
  <label for="username">Username</label>
  <input
   type="text"
   id="username"
   class="form-control"
   ngModel
   name="username"
   required
  />
 </div>
 <button class="btn btn-primary" type="submit">Submit</button>
</form>
```


//typescript file

```typescript
import { Component , ViewChild } from '@angular/core';

import { NgForm } from '@angular/forms';

@Component({
 selector: 'app-root',
 templateUrl: './app.component.html',
 styleUrls: ['./app.component.css']
})
export class AppComponent {
 @ViewChild(' formData ') formObject: NgForm;

 onSubmit() {
 console.log('submitted form values : ' + this.formObject);
```

```
    }
}
```

2. Reactive Forms

Reactive forms provide model driven approach to handle user inputs.

- Libraries which needs to be imported for reactive forms
    1. ReactiveFormsModule
    2. FormGroup
    3. FormControl
    4. Validators (optional :- for validation purpose)

1. Declaring form objects in typescript file (.ts file)

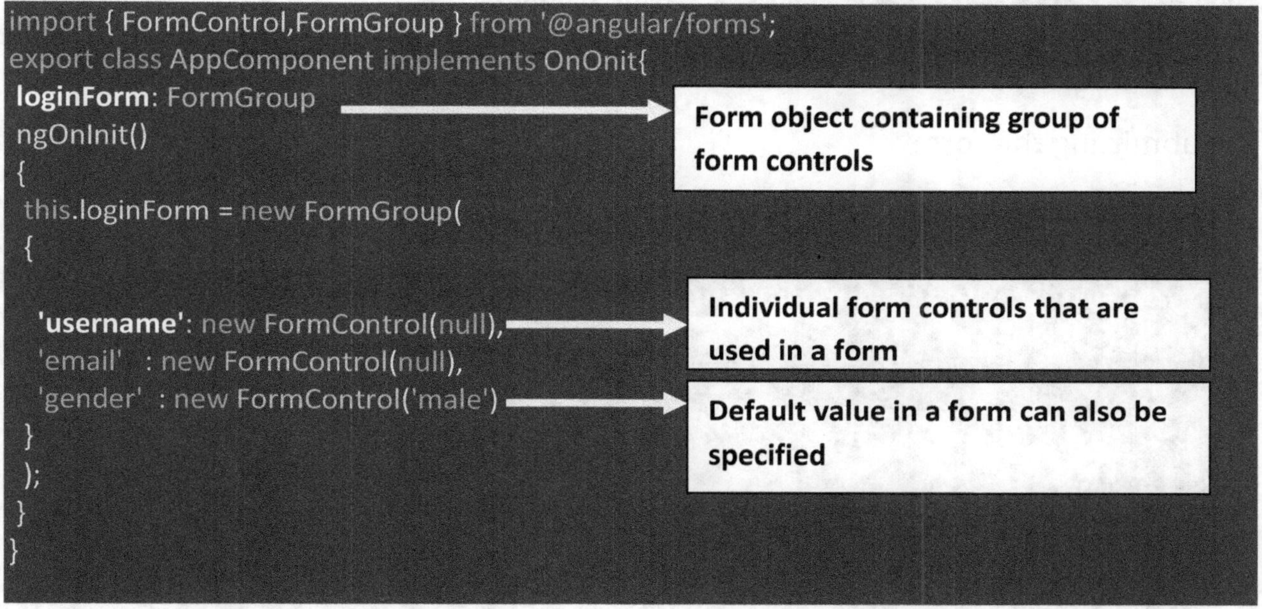

FormControl are key value pairs in which arguments can be passed

1st argument - default value

2nd argument - validators

3rd argument - asyncvalidators

2. Synching Typescript and Html Form Objects (.html file)

```html
<form [formGroup]="loginForm" (ngSubmit)="Submit()">
  <input
    id="username"
    formControlName="username"
  />
</form>
```

value of 'loginForm' is passed from typescript to html using Property binding

It's a same form control name that is used in typescript file. Using this we can access all data of this element

3. Submitting the form

// html file

```html
<form [formGroup]="loginForm" (ngSubmit)="Submit()">
  <input
    id="username"
    formControlName=" username "
  />
</form>
```

ngSubmit event is fired which call the 'Submit()' method in a typescript file

//typescript file

```typescript
import { FormControl,FormGroup } from '@angular/forms';
export class AppComponent implements OnOnit{
loginForm: FormGroup
ngOnInit()
{
 this.loginForm = new FormGroup(
 {
```

```
  'username' : new FormControl(null),
   'email'   : new FormControl(null),
   'gender'  : new FormControl('male')
 }
);
}
 Submit(): void {
   console.log(this.loginForm );  ────────▶  Can access all form controls and values
}
```

4.Adding Validations

- Pass Validators as 2nd argument in FormControl
- **Validators** needs to be imported '@angular/forms'

```
import { FormControl,FormGroup , Validators } from '@angular/forms';

{
this.loginForm = new FormGroup
({
 'username':  new FormControl(null , Validators.required ),     ◀── Required field validation is applied on this control
//Passing multiple validators - Passed as array
'email':  new FormControl(null ,[ Validators.required, Validators.email ])
) };
}
```

Multiple Validations :- Required field and email validation is applied on this control

5. Getting access to controls in Html template

- **get()** :- Get access to controls, by specifying control name or its path.
- e.g.:- loginForm.get('username')

```
<span
*ngIf="!loginForm.get('username').valid && loginForm.get('username').touched"
```

```
> Validation message
</span>
```

Reset the form

```
this.loginForm.reset()
```

18.1 Validity States

1. **ng-invalid** - if the field doesn't satisfy validation requirements
2. **ng-valid** - if the field satisfies validation requirements
3. **ng-dirty** - if field values are changed
4. **ng-pristine** - if field values are not changed
5. **ng-touched** - if the field is focused
6. **ng-untouched** - if the field is not focused

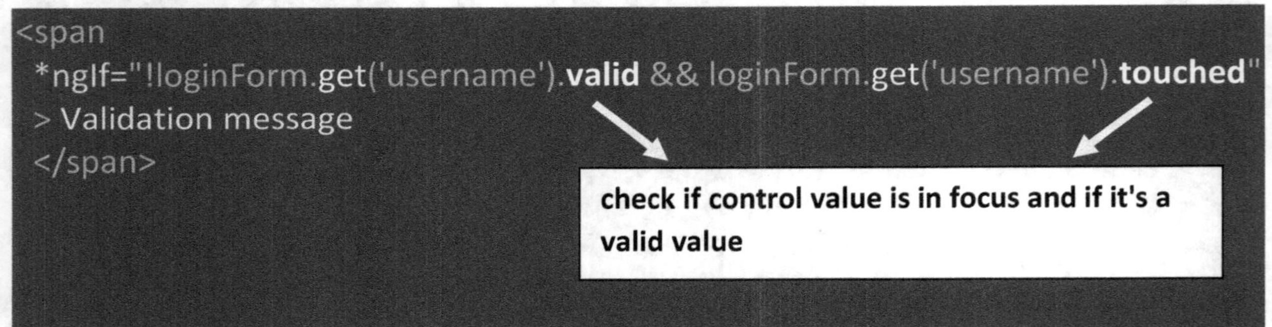

```
<span
 *ngIf="!loginForm.get('username').valid && loginForm.get('username').touched"
> Validation message
</span>
```

19. Routing

Routes are objects comprised of at least one path and a component

Routes are objects in which parameters are passed as a key value pairs

1. **Path** - refers to the URL of the component
2. **Component** - refers to the component corresponding to a URL specified in path

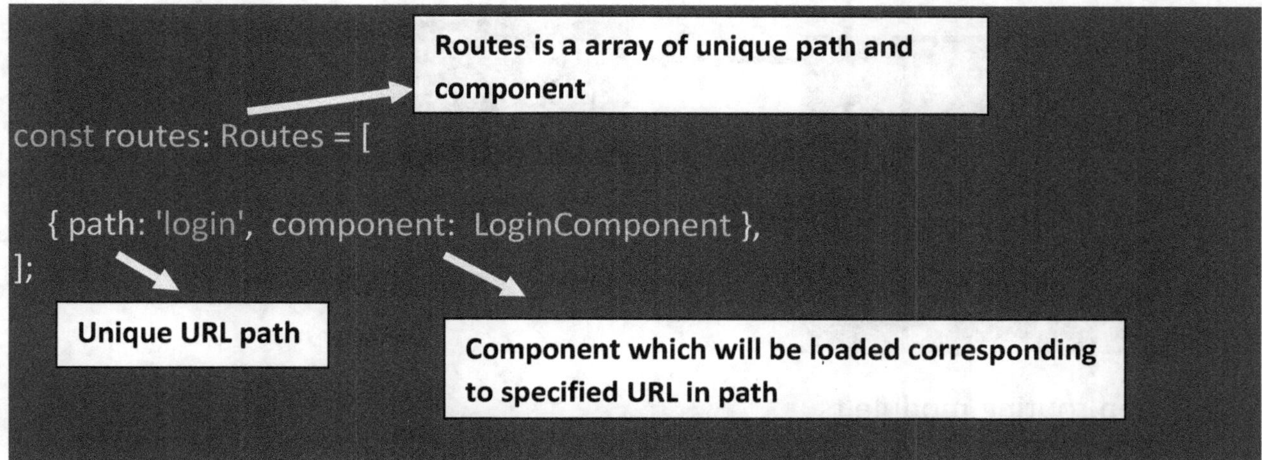

1. Register routes

Libraries that needs to be imported for Routing to work :-

1. Routes from '@angular/router'
2. RouterModule from '@angular/router'

```
import { Routes, RouterModule } from '@angular/router';
```

These libraries are usually imported at highest level to provide application level scope.

- Mostly we register routes in AppModule

- Separate Routing Module can also be used to register routing paths

In newer Angular versions, we get an option to add a separate Routing module at the time of creating new project.

```
E:\WS\Angular WS>ng new test
? Would you like to add Angular routing? (y/N)
```

if you choose 'y' as an option, then a separate routing module will be added to your project.

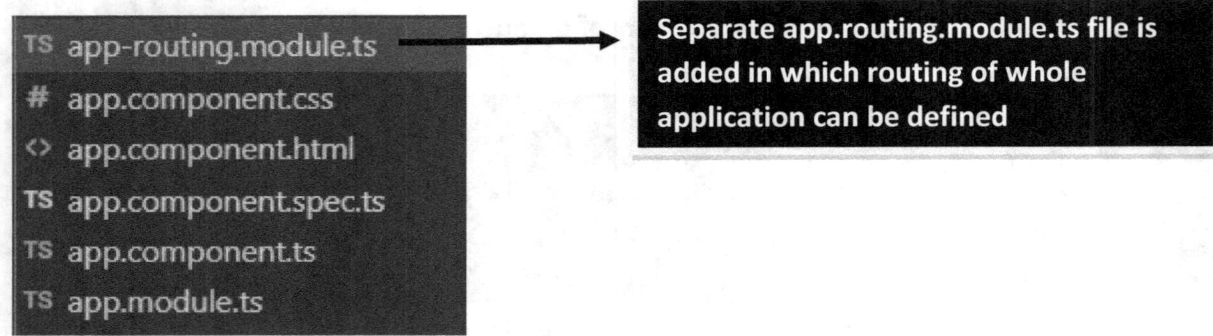

e.g. : - app.routing.module.ts

```
import { LoginComponent } from './login/login.component';
import { NgModule } from '@angular/core';
import { Routes, RouterModule } from '@angular/router';
import { AppComponent } from './app.component';

const routes: Routes = [
  { path: 'login', component: LoginComponent}
];

@NgModule({
 imports: [RouterModule.forRoot(routes)],
 exports: [RouterModule]
})
export class AppRoutingModule { }
```

- unique URLs are defined in Routes array
- These routes array needs to be registered in imports array of NgModule using **RouterModule.forRoot(routes)**

Now, this routing module can be added to appModule which will provide a application level scope to routes.

<u>AppModule.ts</u>

```typescript
import { BrowserModule } from '@angular/platform-browser';
import { NgModule } from '@angular/core';
import { AppRoutingModule } from './app-routing.module';
import { AppComponent } from './app.component';
import { LoginComponent } from './login/login.component';

@NgModule({
  declarations: [
    AppComponent,
    LoginComponent
  ],
  imports: [
    BrowserModule,
    AppRoutingModule,
  ],
  providers: [],
  bootstrap: [AppComponent]
})
export class AppModule { }
```

> **AppRoutingModule now can be included in imports array . Now all routes defined in AppRoutingModule will be available for whole application**

2. Add Placeholder in component

After registering routes, we need to a add placeholder in a parent component to load different components

<router-outlet></router-outlet> is a placeholder

Content of Activated component will be loaded inside the **router-outlet** placeholder

e.g. :- We have AppComponent as our root parent component in which all child components will be loaded.

So, we can add a placeholder in the template of AppComponent where templates of child components will be loaded

App.component.ts

```typescript
import { Component, OnInit } from '@angular/core';

@Component({
  selector: 'app-root',
  templateUrl: './app.component.html',
  styleUrls: ['./app.component.css'],
})
export class AppComponent implements OnInit {

  constructor() {

  }
  ngOnInit(): void {

  }
}
```

App.component.html

```
<div>
<router-outlet></router-outlet>
</div>
```

It works as a placeholder in which content of all child components will be loaded

3. RouterLink

Links of routes can be added using RouterLink

URL specified in routerLink will do pattern matching of this path in router module and will load corresponding component accordingly

e.g. :-

```
<a routerLink = "login">Login</a>
```

routerLink is a directive which is used to traverse the URL path

Now, in the <a> element we can also use href to load route links. But we use routerLink instead of href because of following reasons :-

- RouterLink is faster than href
- RouterLink avoids reloading of page while in href page gets reloaded and all the storages of the page will get lost

routerLink can also be used in property binding

```
<a [routerLink]="['/login']">Login</a>
```

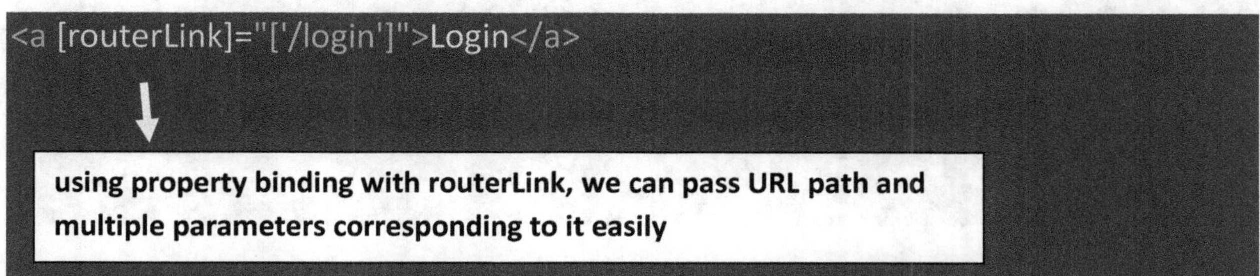

using property binding with routerLink, we can pass URL path and multiple parameters corresponding to it easily

<u>**4.RouterLinkActive**</u>

Now, using routerLink we can traverse to different routes but we will not be able to know which route is currently active .

e.g.:-

Now, let's say we have defined three router Links and we also getting expected output but out of three links , we don't know which one is active.

```html
<div>
 <ul class="nav nav-tabs">
  <li>
   <a class="nav-link"
   routerLink="link1"
   >
   Link1</a>
  </li>
  <li>
   <a class="nav-link"
   routerLink="link2"
   >
   Link2</a>
  </li>
  <li>
   <a class="nav-link"
   routerLink="link3"
   >
   Link3</a>
  </li>
 </ul>
</div>
<div></div>
<router-outlet></router-outlet>
```

Output

Link1   Link2   Link3

link1 works!

Now, to add some styling to this route links , we will be using **routeLinkActive** directive.

Using it we can set the selected route link as active

e.g:-

```html
<div>
 <ul class="nav nav-tabs">
  <li>
   <a class="nav-link"
   routerLink="link1"
   routerLinkActive="active">
   Link1</a>
  </li>
  <li>
   <a class="nav-link"
   routerLink="link2"
   routerLinkActive="active">
   Link2</a>
  </li>
  <li>
   <a class="nav-link"
   routerLink="link3"
   routerLinkActive="active">
   Link3</a>
  </li>
 </ul>
</div>
<div></div>
```

```
<router-outlet></router-outlet>
```

Output

Link1   Link2   Link3

link2 works!

Now, as you can see the color of selected link tab is changed. We now know which routing tab is selected

you can check which tab is selected in developer tools as well

```
▼<li _ngcontent-wix-c19>
    <a _ngcontent-wix-c19 routerlink="link1" routerlinkactive="active" class=
    "nav-link" ng-reflect-router-link="link1" ng-reflect-router-link-active=
    "active" href="/link1"> Link1</a>
  </li>
▼<li _ngcontent-wix-c19>
    <a _ngcontent-wix-c19 routerlink="link2" routerlinkactive="active" class=
    "nav-link active" ng-reflect-router-link="link2" ng-reflect-router-link-
    active="active" href="/link2"> Link2</a>
  </li>
▼<li _ngcontent-wix-c19>
    <a _ngcontent-wix-c19 routerlink="link3" routerlinkactive="active" class=
    "nav-link" ng-reflect-router-link="link3" ng-reflect-router-link-active=
    "active" href="/link3"> Link3</a> == $0
  </li>
```


As you can see in the figure, we have a active class in link2 and rest of the links do not have active class.

routerLinkActiveOptions :

if we are giving some default path in our routing like "/" then we need to tell angular that link should get active for this particular path only

```
<li [routerLinkActiveOptions]="{exact:true}"><a routerLinkActive="active" routerLink="/">
Login</a></li>
```

<u>**5. Navigate**</u>

We can also navigate programmatically from typescript file. Let's say we need to load certain routes based on some conditions then in that case we can use **navigate** .

e.g.:-

Now, let say we have button in link1 page using which we want to navigate to link2, then we can use **navigate** method .

Link1   Link2   Link3

link1 works!

Link2

link1.component.html

```html
<p>link1 works!</p>
<p>
  <button class="btn btn-primary" (click)="OnSubmit()">Link2</button>
</p>
```

link1.component.ts

```typescript
import { Component, OnInit } from '@angular/core';
import { Router } from '@angular/router';

@Component({
  selector: 'app-link1',
  templateUrl: './link1.component.html',
  styles: []
```

```typescript
})
export class Link1Component implements OnInit {

  constructor(private router: Router) { }

    ngOnInit(): void {
  }

  OnSubmit(): void
  {
      this.router.navigate(['link2']);
  }
}
```

using navigate method we can traverse to specified route

Steps to use Navigate

1. import router from '@angular/router'

```typescript
import { Router } from '@angular/router';
```

2. Inject Router in a constructor

```typescript
constructor(private router: Router) { }
```

3. Use router instance to call navigate method

```typescript
this.router.navigate(['link2']);
```

<u>**Activated route**</u>

It signifies the currently active route

```
import { Component, OnInit } from '@angular/core';
import { ActivatedRoute, Router } from '@angular/router';

@Component({
  selector: 'app-link1',
  templateUrl: './link1.component.html',
  styles: [],
})
export class Link1Component implements OnInit {
  constructor(private router: Router, private activeRoute: ActivatedRoute) {}

  ngOnInit(): void {}

  OnSubmit(): void {
    this.router.navigate(['link2']);
  }
  OnReload(): void {
    this.router.navigate(['/link1'], { relativeTo: this.activeRoute });
  }
}
```

Pass 2nd parameter in navigate method which is a java script object.

pass relativeTo as key and the currently active route as its value

Steps to use **ActivatedRoute** :-

1. import ActivatedRoute from @angular/router'

```
import { ActivatedRoute, Router } from '@angular/router';
```

2. Inject ActivatedRoute   in a constructor

```
constructor(private router: Router, private activeRoute: ActivatedRoute) {}
```

3. Use the instance in navigate method

```
this.router.navigate(['/link1'], { relativeTo: this.activeRoute });
```

6. Passing and Fetching Parameters in a route

Routing parameters types

1. Required parameters
2. Optional parameters
3. Query parameters
4. State parameters

1. Required routing parameters

Required parameter in a route can be passed as :-

```
{path: 'link2/:param1', component: Link2Component}
```

Anything passed with a colon (:) is a dynamic parameter. In this case :param1 is a dynamic parameter.

Dynamic parameter :-

- Dynamic parameter means that parameter name is not dependent while navigating the route. Any parameter can be used while calling route
- Colon (:) is used before parameter name to make it as dynamic parameter

e.g.: -

Let's say we want to pass a parameter from link1 page to page2 .

Scenario : - If user clicks Link2 button then the name written in textbox should be passed to link2 page

Output 1

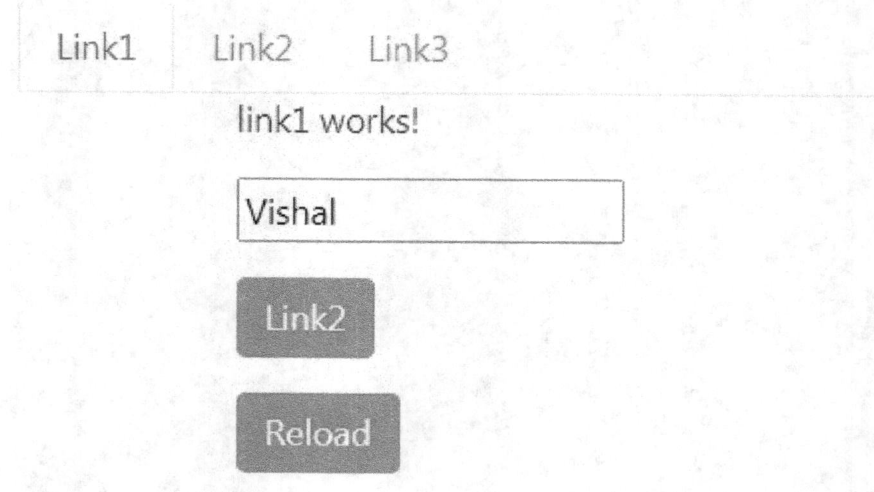

Output 2

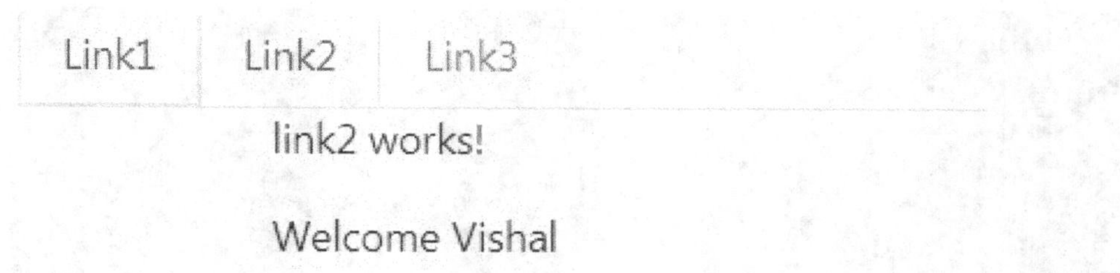

Steps :-

1. Add dynamic parameters

app.routing.module.ts

```
import { Link1Component } from './link1/link1.component';
```

```typescript
import { NgModule } from '@angular/core';
import { Routes, RouterModule } from '@angular/router';
import { Link2Component } from './link2/link2.component';
import { Link3Component } from './link3/link3.component';

const routes: Routes = [
  {path: 'link1', component: Link1Component},
  {path: 'link2', component: Link2Component},
  {path: 'link2/:param1', component: Link2Component},
  {path: 'link3', component: Link3Component},
];

@NgModule({
  imports: [RouterModule.forRoot(routes)],
  exports: [RouterModule]
})
export class AppRoutingModule { }
```

2. Pass route parameters

link1.component.ts

```typescript
import { Component, OnInit } from '@angular/core';
import { ActivatedRoute, Router } from '@angular/router';

@Component({
  selector: 'app-link1',
  templateUrl: './link1.component.html',
  styles: [],
})
export class Link1Component implements OnInit {
  constructor(private router: Router, private activeRoute: ActivatedRoute) {}

  username: string;
  ngOnInit(): void {}
```

```
OnSubmit(): void {
  this.router.navigate(['link2', this.username]);
}
OnReload(): void {
  this.router.navigate(['/link1'], { relativeTo: this.activeRoute });
}
}
```


link1.component.html

```
<p>link1 works!</p>
<p><input type="text" placeholder="default" [(ngModel)]="username"></p>
<p>
 <button class="btn btn-primary" (click)="OnSubmit()">Link2</button>
</p>
<p>
 <button class="btn btn-primary" (click)="OnReload()">Reload</button>
</p>
```

We are using 'username' as a variable in which we are binding value of textbox and this username is passed as parameter in navigate method.

3. Fetch route parameters

snapshot :- Get access to currently active routes' parameters

Snapshot is one of a way to fetch parameters from currently active route

ActivatedRoute :- Get access to currently active route

e.g. :

In this case we have link2 as our destination page/route

link2.component.html

```
<p>link2 works!</p>
```

```html
<p>Welcome {{name}} </p>
```
(link2.component.ts)

```typescript
import { Component, OnInit } from '@angular/core';
import { ActivatedRoute } from '@angular/router';

@Component({
  selector: 'app-link2',
  templateUrl: './link2.component.html',
  styles: [

  ]
})
export class Link2Component implements OnInit {

  constructor(private activatedRoute: ActivatedRoute) { }
  name = this.activatedRoute.snapshot.params['param1'];

  ngOnInit(): void {
  }
}
```


(app.routing.module.ts)

```typescript
{path: 'link2/:param1', component: Link2Component},
```

Note :-

In a new versions of Angular , parameters can be fetched as :-

```typescript
name = this.activatedRoute.snapshot.params.param1;
```

Fetch route parameters reactively

- snapshot is appropriate to fetch first initialization of route parameters
- For successive changes Params observable should be used

Syntax :-

```
this.activatedRoute.params
  .subscribe(
  (params: Params) => {
    //Fetch route parameters here...
  }
  );
```

Let's see a scenario for better understanding :-

Output 1

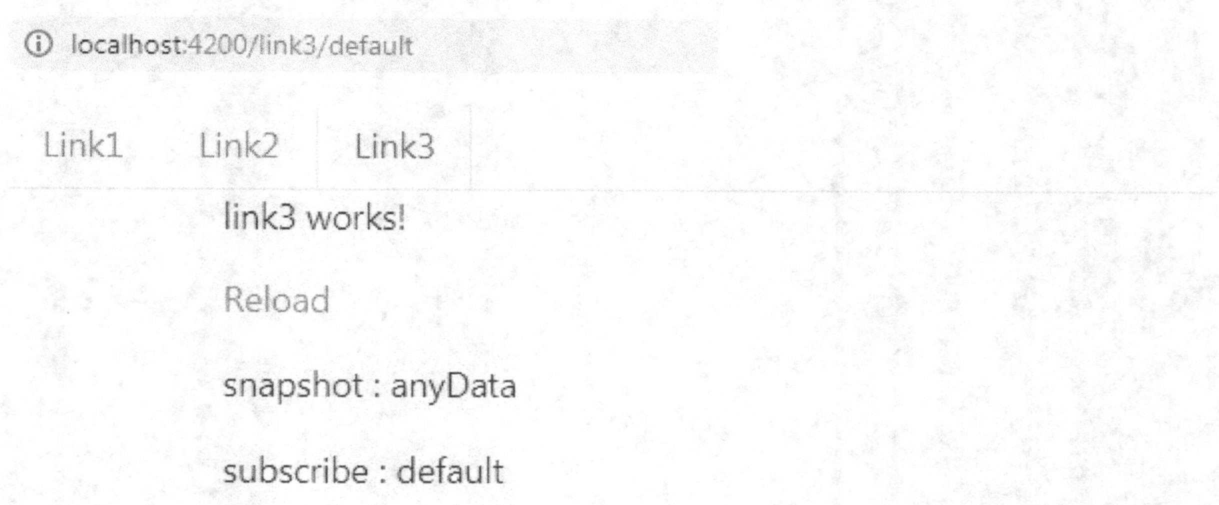

We have link3 page and in this we have Reload page link.

using **snapshot** we will be getting first initialized data only. Once we reload this page we will still be getting this value and our default value is not updated

To fetch updated values we need to use **Params** observable

link3.component.html

```
<p>link3 works!</p>
<p>
```

```html
<a [routerLink]="['/link3','default']">Reload</a>
</p>
<p>snapshot : {{snapshotData}} </p>
<p>subscribe : {{subscribeData}} </p>
```


link3.component.ts

```typescript
import { Component, OnInit } from '@angular/core';
import { ActivatedRoute, Params } from '@angular/router';

@Component({
  selector: 'app-link3',
  templateUrl: './link3.component.html',
  styles: [],
})
export class Link3Component implements OnInit {
  constructor(private activatedRoute: ActivatedRoute) {}
  subscribeData;
  snapshotData = this.activatedRoute.snapshot.params.param1;

  ngOnInit(): void {
    this.activatedRoute.params.subscribe((params: Params) => {
      this.subscribeData = params.param1;
    });
  }
}
```

As you can see in the output subscribeData is getting updated with default value
while snapshotData is having initialized data.

2. Optional parameters - paramMap

Not mandatory to pass parameter in a routing path while defining them in routing
module

(app-routing.module.ts)

```typescript
import { Link1Component } from './link1/link1.component';
import { NgModule } from '@angular/core';
import { Routes, RouterModule } from '@angular/router';
import { Link2Component } from './link2/link2.component';
import { Link3Component } from './link3/link3.component';
import { Link4Component } from './link4/link4.component';

const routes: Routes = [
 {path: 'link1', component: Link1Component},
 {path: 'link2', component: Link2Component},
 {path: 'link2/:param1', component: Link2Component},
 {path: 'link3', component: Link3Component},
 {path: 'link3/:param1', component: Link3Component},
 {path: 'link4', component: Link4Component},
];

@NgModule({
 imports: [RouterModule.forRoot(routes)],
 exports: [RouterModule]
})
export class AppRoutingModule { }
```


(link1.component.html)

```html
<p>link1 works!</p>
<p><input type="text" placeholder="default" [(ngModel)]="username"></p>
<p>
 <button class="btn btn-primary" (click)="OnSubmit()">Link2</button>
</p>


<p>
 <button class="btn btn-primary" (click)="OnReload()">Reload</button>
</p>
```

```html
<p>
 <a [routerLink]="['link4',{arg1:'value',arg2:'value2',multiValue:['val1','val2','val
3']}]"></a>
</p>
<p>
<button class="btn btn-primary" (click)="OnSubmitLink4()">Link4</button>
</p>
<p>
```

(link1.component.ts)

```typescript
import { Component, OnInit } from '@angular/core';
import { ActivatedRoute, Router } from '@angular/router';

@Component({
 selector: 'app-link1',
 templateUrl: './link1.component.html',
 styles: [],
})
export class Link1Component implements OnInit {
 constructor(private router: Router, private activeRoute: ActivatedRoute) {}

 username: string;
 ngOnInit(): void {}

 OnSubmit(): void {
  this.router.navigate(['link2', this.username]);
 }

 OnReload(): void {
  this.router.navigate(['/link1'], { relativeTo: this.activeRoute });
 }
 OnSubmitLink4(): void {
  this.router.navigate([
   'link4',
```

```
    { arg1: 'value', arg2: 'value2', multiValue: ['val1', 'val2', 'val3'] },
  ]);
 }
}
```

(link4.component.html)

```html
<p>link4 works!</p>
<p><b>optional parameters - using paramMap</b></p>
<p>optional params : {{ getoptionalParam }}</p>
<p>Get all optional params : {{ getAlloptionalParam }}</p>
<p>has optional parameter : {{ hasoptionalParam }}</p>
<p>has optional parameter : {{ hasoptionalParam2 }}</p>
```

(link4.component.ts)

```typescript
import { Component, OnInit } from '@angular/core';
import { ActivatedRoute } from '@angular/router';

@Component({
 selector: 'app-link4',
 templateUrl: './link4.component.html',
 styles: [],
})
export class Link4Component implements OnInit {
 constructor(private activatedRoute: ActivatedRoute) {}
 getoptionalParam;
 getAlloptionalParam;
 hasoptionalParam;
 hasoptionalParam2;
 ngOnInit(): void {
  this.getoptionalParam = this.activatedRoute.snapshot.paramMap.get('arg1');
  this.getAlloptionalParam = this.activatedRoute.snapshot.paramMap.getAll('multiValue');
  this.hasoptionalParam = this.activatedRoute.snapshot.paramMap.has('arg1');
  this.hasoptionalParam2 = this.activatedRoute.snapshot.paramMap.has('arg4');
 }
}
```

(Output)

paramMap

We can use paramMap instead of param to fetch parameters as :-

- It provide more options to fetch parameters like **get(), getAll(), has()**
- **Multiple values** corresponding to a parameter can be fetched using paramMap
- paramMap is used in **newer versions** while param may get depreciated in newer angular versions

paramMap has 3 methods :-

1. **get()** :- it will get the value of specified parameter

```
this.getoptionalParam = this.activatedRoute.snapshot.paramMap.get('arg1');
```

2. **getAll()** :- it will get all values of specified parameter

```
this.getAlloptionalParam = this.activatedRoute.snapshot.paramMap.getAll('m
ultiValue');
```

3. **has()** :- it checks if specified parameter is present in a route

```
this.hasoptionalParam = this.activatedRoute.snapshot.paramMap.has('arg1');
```

3. Optional parameters - queryParamMap

Optional parameters across any route can be passed using query parameters

Output

link1.component.ts

```
OnSubmitQueryParam(): void {
  this.router.navigate(['/link5'], { queryParams: { arg1: 'value1', arg2: 'value2' , m
ultiValue: ['val1', 'val2', 'val3']} });
}
```

queryParams is passed as argument in navigate
method to pass query parameters

link5.component.ts

```typescript
this.getqueryParam = this.activatedRoute.snapshot.queryParamMap.get('arg1');

this.getAllqueryParam = this.activatedRoute.snapshot.queryParamMap.getAll('multiValue');

this.hasqueryParam = this.activatedRoute.snapshot.queryParamMap.has('arg1');
```

4. State Parameters

In new Angular versions we can also pass parameters in a route by using 2nd argument of navigation method in which we can pass navigation extras

- **Passing state parameters**

```typescript
this.router.navigate(['/link1/child1'], {state: {arg1: id}});
```

In a state we can pass parameters with a route link

- **Fetching state parameters**

```typescript
constructor(private router: Router) {
    this.id = this.router.getCurrentNavigation().extras.state['arg1'];
}
```

We will be using getCurrentNavigation() method to fetch state parameters from a route.

points to remember

- **Import Router from '@angular/router'**

```typescript
import { Router } from '@angular/router';
```

- **Constructor should be used to fetch state parameters**

in newer versions argument is passed a property rather than a literal

```
constructor(private router: Router) {
    this.id = this.router.getCurrentNavigation().extras.state.arg2;
}
```

19.1 Routing Fragments

- The fragments are optional part of a URL prefixed with a hash (#) symbol
- It is generally used to identify some portion of the URL

Pass fragments
- Passing fragment in html

```
<a [routerLink]="['/link7']" fragment="fragmentData">Link7 - fragments</a>
```

- Passing fragment programmatically

```
this.router.navigate(['/link7'], { fragment: 'fragmentData' });
```

Output URL

ⓘ localhost:4200/link7#fragmentData

Fetch fragments

Fetch fragment using **snapshot**
- It will fetch the fragment at the time of initialization of URL

```
this.fragmentParam = this.activatedRoute.snapshot.fragment;
```

Fetch fragment using **subscribe**

- It will fetch the fragment reactively i.e. every time there is a change in fragment, it will fetch updated fragment

```
this.activatedRoute.fragment.subscribe((fragment: string) => {
this.fragmentSubscribe = fragment;
});
```

7. Child routes

We can also load child components inside parent components by using children property in route configuration.

19.2 children :-

It's a Array of child route objects that specifies a nested route configuration

```
path: 'link1',
    component: Link1Component,
    children: [
        { path: 'child1', component: Child1Component},
        { path: 'child2', component: Child2Component},
    ]
```

A placeholder needs to be added in parent component where you want to load a child component

```
<router-outlet></router-outlet>
```

Add <router-outlet> in a parent component.

This child route can be called in following way :-

```
this.router.navigate(['/link1/child1'],{state:{arg1: id}});
```

8. Wild card routes

19.3 Wild card Route

To handle any route which is not defined in routes config, we can use wild card (**) routing to handle undefined routes.

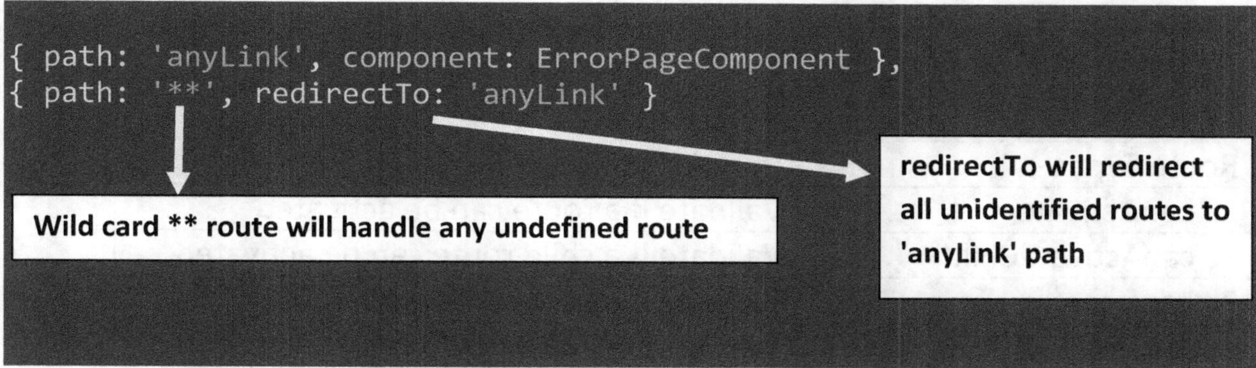

> **Points to remember : -**
- Routes are parsed from top to bottom
- Generic routes like '**' should be placed in last

20. Route Guards

- Router Guards allows or disallows access to route navigations
- Router Guards are executed before a route is loaded or before leaving any route

There are 4 types of routing guards :-

Route Types	Description
1. canActivate	Validate If a route can be activated
2. canActivateChild	Validate If a child route can be activated
3. canDeactivate	Validate If a user can leave a route
4. Resolve	Load certain data before route is loaded

1. canActivate

Steps to add route guard in your application :-

1. Add route guard file in your application.

CLI command to add a guard in application

```
ng g guard route
```

Output Filename :- route.guard.ts

Generate guard without .spec file

```
ng g guard --skiptests=true  route
```

Example of route guard :-

<u>(route.guard.ts)</u>

```ts
import { Injectable } from '@angular/core';
import {
  CanActivate,
  ActivatedRouteSnapshot,
  RouterStateSnapshot,
  UrlTree,
} from '@angular/router';
import { Observable } from 'rxjs';

@Injectable({
  providedIn: 'root',
})
export class RouteGuard implements CanActivate {
  canActivate(
    next: ActivatedRouteSnapshot,
    state: RouterStateSnapshot
  ):
    | Observable<boolean | UrlTree>
    | Promise<boolean | UrlTree>
    | boolean
    | UrlTree {
    return true;
  }
}
```

Step 2 : Now, we need to define which routes needs to be protected by this route guard.

(app-routing.module.ts)

```ts
{
    path: 'link1',
    canActivate: [RouteGuard],
    component: Link1Component,
    children: [
      { path: 'child1', component: Child1Component},
      { path: 'child2', component: Child2Component}
    ],
},
```

canActivate property is added in route config to provide route guard for a particular route.

Now, RouteGuard will always be activated before 'link1' route is loaded and you can apply any authorization or business logic in RouteGuard that you want to activate before route is loaded.

2. canActivateChild

canActivateChild protects all child routes
Implementation is same as canActivate

(route-child.guard.ts)

```typescript
import { Injectable } from '@angular/core';
import {
  CanActivate,
  ActivatedRouteSnapshot,
  RouterStateSnapshot,
  UrlTree, CanActivateChild
} from '@angular/router';
import { Observable } from 'rxjs';

@Injectable({
  providedIn: 'root',
})
export class RouteChildGuard implements CanActivate , CanActivateChild
{
  canActivateChild(childRoute: ActivatedRouteSnapshot, state: RouterStateSnapshot):
    boolean | UrlTree | Observable<boolean | UrlTree> | Promise<boolean
  | UrlTree> {
    return false;
  }

  canActivate(
    next: ActivatedRouteSnapshot,
    state: RouterStateSnapshot
  ):
    | Observable<boolean | UrlTree>
```

```
      | Promise<boolean | UrlTree>
      | boolean
      | UrlTree {
    return true;
  }
}
```

In this, we e implementing canActivateChild method which is implemented from
CanActivateChild interface.
In this canActivateChild method we can apply authorization or business logic for
child routes

Now, we need to add canActivateChild hook in route config as well

```
{
    path: 'guard',
    component: RouteGuardComponent,
    canActivateChild: [RouteChildGuard],
    children: [
      { path: ':id', component: RouteGuardComponent },
      { path: ':id/:name', component: RouteGuardComponent },
    ],
}
```

In this RouteChildGuard will protect all the child routes defined in this route.

3. canDeactivate

canDeactivate guard is activated before leaving any route. Suppose we want to
add some business logic before user navigates away from current route then in
that case we can use **canDeactivate** guard.

Steps :-

1. Add a canDeactivate guard file in your application.

e.g.:-

```typescript
import { Injectable } from '@angular/core';
import {
  CanDeactivate,
  ActivatedRouteSnapshot,
  RouterStateSnapshot,
  UrlTree,
  Router, ActivatedRoute
} from '@angular/router';
import { Observable } from 'rxjs';

@Injectable({
  providedIn: 'root',
})
export class CanDeactivateGuard implements CanDeactivate<unknown> {
  constructor(private router: Router, private route: ActivatedRoute) {
}

  canDeactivate(
    component: unknown,
    currentRoute: ActivatedRouteSnapshot,
    currentState: RouterStateSnapshot,
    nextState?: RouterStateSnapshot
  ):
    | Observable<boolean | UrlTree>
    | Promise<boolean | UrlTree>
    | boolean
    | UrlTree {
    const result = confirm('Are you sure want to leave this page?');
    if (result === false) {
      this.router.navigate([currentState.url]);
    }
    return true;
  }
}
```

In this example, we have implemented canDeactivate method of CanDeactivate
interface. In canDeactivate we can have our business logic while will be loaded
just before user navigates away from the current route.

2. Add canDeactivate hook in routing config

```
{
    path: 'guard',
    component: RouteGuardComponent,
    canActivateChild: [RouteChildGuard],
    canDeactivate: [CanDeactivateGuard],
    children: [
      { path: ':id', component: RouteGuardComponent },
      { path: ':id/:name', component: RouteGuardComponent },
    ],
}
```

Now when user tries to navigate away from this route (i.e. 'guard') then canDeactivateGuard gets loaded and all its business logic will be executed.

4. Resolve

- Resolve data before route navigation
- Pre-load certain data before route navigation

Steps:-

1. Add resolve guard in your application

e.g.

(resolve.guard.ts)

```
import {
  Resolve,
  ActivatedRouteSnapshot,
  RouterStateSnapshot,
} from '@angular/router';
import { Injectable } from '@angular/core';
import { Observable } from 'rxjs';

@Injectable(
  {
    providedIn: 'root'
  }
)
export class ResolveGuard implements Resolve<string> {
```

```
resolve(
  route: ActivatedRouteSnapshot,
  state: RouterStateSnapshot
): Observable<string> | Promise<string>  {
  return route.params.name;
  }
 }
}
```

In resolve guard we can actually do some data manipulation and return some kind
of data.

2. Add resolve hook in route object of routing module file.
(app-routing.module.ts)

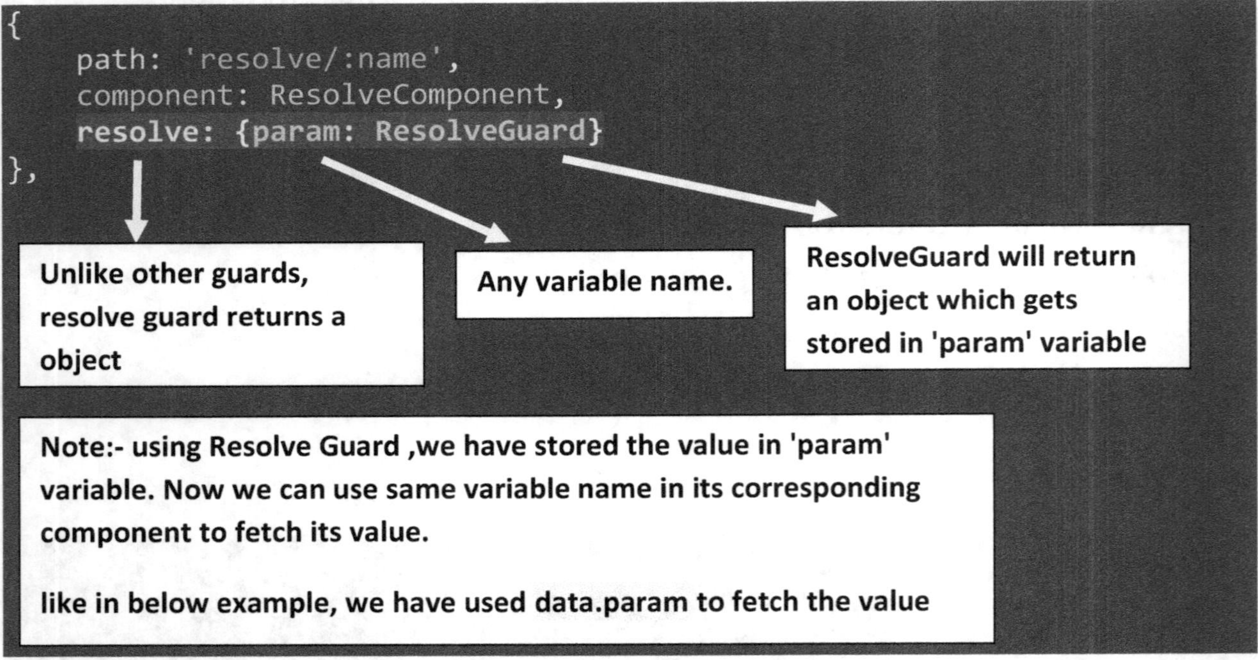

3. Fetch data in component associated with resolve guard.
(resolve.component.ts)

```
import { Component, OnInit } from '@angular/core';
import { ActivatedRoute, Data } from '@angular/router';

@Component({
  selector: 'app-resolve',
  templateUrl: './resolve.component.html',
```

```
  styles: [],
})
export class ResolveComponent implements OnInit {
  constructor(private route: ActivatedRoute) {}

  ngOnInit(): void {

    this.route.data.subscribe((data: Data) => {
      alert('Welcome ' + data.param);
    });
  }
}
```

> **This variable name i.e. 'param' in this case should be same as we have used in resolve hook in route config**
>
> ```
> resolve: {param: ResolveGuard}
> ```

- In this we are using **Data** type which can be imported from '@angular/router'
- **Data** type is used to fetch static or dynamic data from routes

<u>fetch static data from route using **Data** :-</u>
(app-routing.module.ts)

```
{ path: 'error', component: PageNotFoundComponent,
  data: {message: 'Page navigation error!'} },
```

> **In the data type we can pass any static data**

(component.ts)

```
this.message = this.route.snapshot.data['message'];
```

> **using data type we can fetch static data from this route. Like in this case data stored in 'message' variable is fetched**

21. Observables

- An Observable is a data source which emits multiple values asynchronously coming from sources like Http requests, events, user input etc.
- Values from Observable are pushed to observers
- Typically asynchronous operations are handled by using Observable
- Lazy loading i.e. It will not be called until it is subscribed
- **RxJs** library is used to import Observable
- Can be unsubscribed to prevent memory leaks by using Unsubscribe method
- Observable (publishers/service) push values to observers (subscribers, client)
- The subscribe method **Observable accepts 3 optional functions** as parameters :-

1. **Handle Data** :- Data coming from events raised in sources like Http requests, events, user input etc.
2. **Handle Error** :- Handles any error
3. **Handle Completion** :- Execute any code when Observable is completed

e.g.

```
this.service.getResult()
.subscribe(
    data => this.onSuccess(data),
    error => this.onError(error),
    () => this.onComplete()
);
```

Handles data which is emitted successfully from data sources

Any error can be handled in 2nd parameter successfully from data

3rd parameter will handle the completion tasks

e.g.:-

Like in case of routes, we can also use subscribe method

```
this.route.params.subscribe(
    (data: Params) => {
      console.log('Data: ' + data.id);
    },
    (error) => {
      console.log('Error :' + error);
    },
    () => {
      console.log('Completed...');
    }
);
```

22. RxJs Operators

- RxJs Operators are just function that performs some data manipulations
- RxJs Operators performs action on observable input and returns an observable
- These are pipeable operators i.e. they can be concatenated with subscribe method to get a manipulated output
- RxJs Operators can be imported from 'rxjs/operators' library
- Some of commonly used RxJs Operators are map, filter, tap etc.

1. Map
- map takes observable as input, perform manipulation on it and returns a new manipulated observable as output
- map **transforms** the emitted values from observable
- map is a **pipeable operator**
- import map from 'rxjs/operators'

e.g.:-

In the example below, we are manipulating observable data and then we are subscribing that manipulated data

```
this.route.params.pipe(
    map((data: Params) => 'Data ' + data.id
))
  .subscribe(
    (data) => {
      console.log(data);
    },
    (error) => {
      console.log('Error :' + error);
    },
    () => {
      console.log('Completed...');
    }
  );
```

This map operator will take params observable as input and returns a manipulated data

2. Filter

- Filter operator will apply some filtration before subscribing the data
- import filter from 'rxjs/operators'

Like in the example below we have applied filter operator to send filtered data to subscribe method

```
this.route.params.pipe(
    filter((data: Params) => data.id > 4 ),
    map((data: Params) => 'Data ' + data.id
))
  .subscribe(
    (data) => {
      console.log(data);
    },
    (error) => {
      console.log('Error :' + error);
    },
    () => {
      console.log('Completed...');
    }
  );
```

Operator Chaining :- Multiple operators can be chained together to send the desired output to subscribe method

The filter operator will pass filtered data i.e. id which is greater than 4 to map operator and then to subscribe method.

IF we have id less than or equal to 4 then it will not be passed to map operator and to subscribe method.

3. Tap

- tap takes observable as input, perform manipulation on it and returns same observable as output
- Purpose of tap is to perform some action without manipulating an observable data
- import tap from 'rxjs/operators'

e.g.:

```
this.route.params.pipe(
    filter((data: Params) => data.id > 4 ),
    map((data: Params) => 'Data ' + data.id),
    tap((data) => console.log('Result is :' + data))
)
.subscribe(
    (data) => {
      console.log(data);
    },
    (error) => {
      console.log('Error :' + error);
    },
    () => {
      console.log('Completed...');
    }
);
```

In this example tap operator is used to display the result without manipulation it. observable data is filtered first with filter operator, then that data is manipulated using map operator and lastly tap operator is applied to display the data.

In every application , a backend database source is always required. But we do not interact with databases directly to prevent security issues. Instead we use API services for interaction with Database services .Our Angular application will then interact with API services with the help of Http Requests.

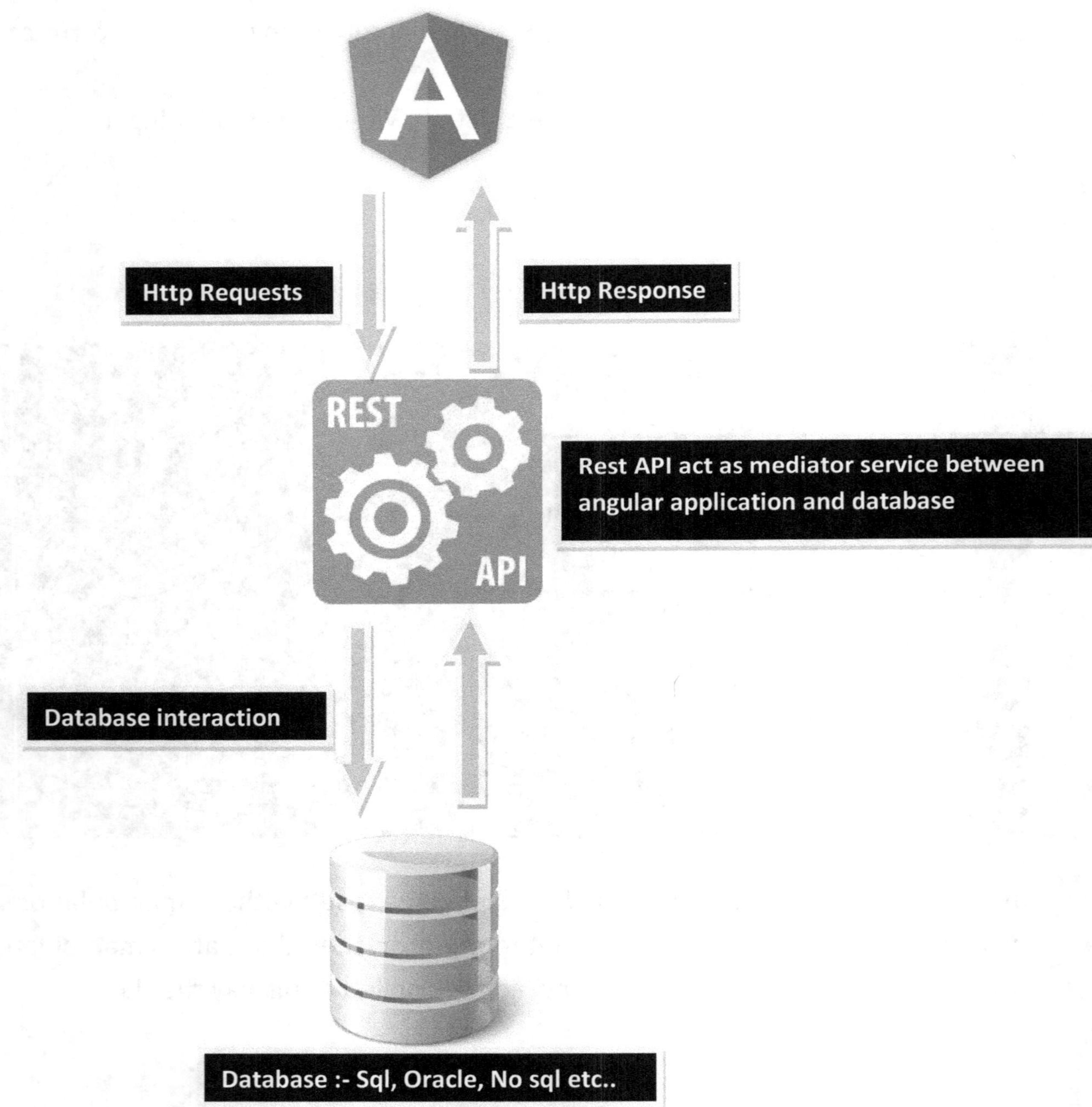

Steps required to use Http requests in angular application :-

1. Import HttpClientModule in App module class

```
import {HttpClientModule} from '@angular/common/http';
```

2. Add this module in imports array to make it available in whole application

```
imports: [
    BrowserModule,
    AppRoutingModule,
    HttpClientModule,
        ],
```

Now, after making HttpClientModule available for whole application , we need to inject the Http Service in a component where we want to use Http Requests

3. We first need to import **HttpClient** from '@angular/common/http'

```
import { HttpClient } from '@angular/common/http';
```

4. Then, we can inject **HttpClient** in our constructor to use all the functionalities of a **HttpClient** in a component.

```
constructor(private http: HttpClient) {}
```

Http request **verbs** :-

1. Post
2. Get
3. Put
4. Delete

1. Post

We use Post requests to add new data in our database

1. In Http post requests, we have 2 required parameters

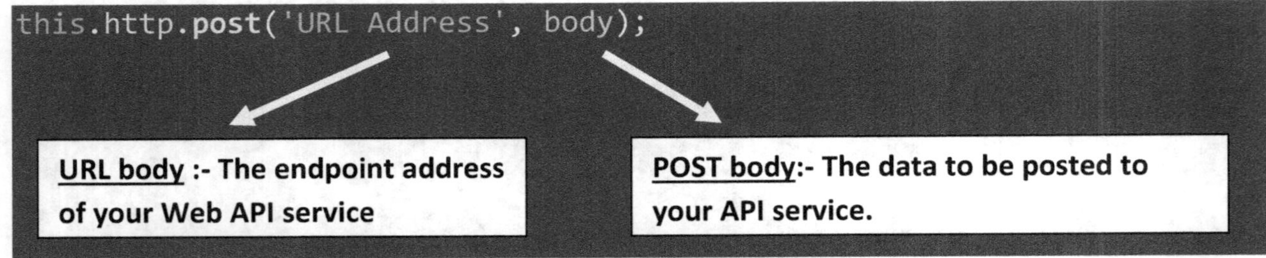

2. Post requests returns an observable which needs to be subscribed in order to use the data response from API service
3. Without subscribing a Http post request, Angular will not even send this post request

e.g.: - In the below example, we have a register method in which we are sending a Http post request to our API service
(e.g.:- Any Service class like myService.ts)

```
register()
{
    const body =
    {
       UserName: this.fomModel.value.UserName,
       Email: this.fomModel.value.Email,
    };

    return this.http.post('http://localhost:8080/api/Register', body);
}
```

Now, In Angular without subscribing , it will not even send a post request.
So, now we will call this register() method and subscribe it.

```
this.service.register().subscribe(
    (res: any) => {
      console.log('Response data is : ' + res);
    }
  );
```

So, like in above example we are subscribing a post request. Now, a post request will be send to a API server.

2. Get

Using Get request, we fetch the data from our database via Api service

- Only 1 parameter is required in Get request

```
this.http.get('http://localhost:8080/api/GetData')
```

URL of web API service from which you want to get your data

- Like Post Requests, we also need to **subscribe** Get requests in order to get any response from web API service

```
this.http.get('http://localhost:8080/api/GetData').subscribe(res => {
  console.log(res);
});
```

Only after subscribing, we will be able to get response from API , otherwise we will not be getting any response.

3. Delete

Delete request is used to delete any data from database.

- Only 1 parameter is required in Get request

```
this.http.delete('http://localhost:8080/api/ClearData')
```

- Again, we need to **subscribe** it to get response from API service

```
this.http.delete('http://localhost:8080/api/ClearData')
.subscribe(res=> {console.log(res);
});
```

4. Put

We use Put requests to update any data in our database via Api

- 2 Parameters are required in Put requests

```
update()
{
    const body =
    {
      UserName: this.fomModel.value.UserName,
      Email: this.fomModel.value.Email,
    };

    return this.http.put('http://localhost:8080/api/Update', body);
}
```

URL body :- The endpoint address of your Web API service

POST body:- The data to be updated to your API service.

- We need to **subscribe** it in order to get response from Api service

```
this.service.update ().subscribe((res: any) => {
      console.log('Response data is : ' + res);
    }
  );
```

<u>**Setting Custom Headers in Http Requests**</u>

An argument can be passed in all Http Requests (Post, Get, Put, Delete) in which custom header can be defined

- We need to import **HttpHeaders** from '@angular/common/http'

```
return this.http
    .get(
      'http://localhost:8080/api/Update/GetData',
      {
        headers: new HttpHeaders({ 'Custom-Header': 'value' })
      }
    )
```

Key-value pair:- A custom header name is passed as a key while the value of this header is set as key

Similarly, query parameter can also be passed in Http requests

- We need to import **HttpParams** from '@angular/common/http'

```
let myParams = new HttpParams();
myParams = myParams.append('param1');
return this.http
    .get(
      'http://localhost:8080/api/Update/GetData',
      {
        headers: new HttpHeaders({ 'Custom-Header': 'value' }),
        params: myParams
      }
    )
```

24. Interceptors

- Interceptor is a mechanism to00 **intercept incoming requests** or outgoing response
- By intercepting we can **modify the request or response**
- It act as a middleware between Angular application and Api service
- Interceptor will always get activated before a http request is made. So. some common behavior can be added in interceptor which may be required in all Http requests e.g.:- authentication tokens
- Multiple Interceptors can be added in a application and they execute in same order as provided in module.
- Normally used for logging, authentication, caching , etc. purposes

How to add Interceptor in Angular application ?

You can either add interceptor class manually or can use CLI command to add interceptor in your application

CLI command:-

```
ng g interceptor auth
```

CLI command (without test/.spec file)

```
ng g interceptor --skipTests=true auth
```

This will create a following file in your application :-

```
auth.interceptor.ts
```

(auth.interceptor.ts)

```typescript
import { Injectable } from '@angular/core';
import {
  HttpRequest,
  HttpHandler,
  HttpEvent,
  HttpInterceptor,
} from '@angular/common/http';
import { Observable } from 'rxjs';

@Injectable()
export class AuthInterceptor implements HttpInterceptor {
  constructor() {}

  intercept(
    request: HttpRequest<unknown>,
    next: HttpHandler
  ): Observable<HttpEvent<unknown>> {
    // logic here...
    return next.handle(request);
  }
}
```

That is the skeleton of interceptor file. Here you can add your interceptor logic.

Now, we need to tell Angular that we are using a Interceptor service in our application.

3 parameters need to be passed in providers array of AppModule for a interceptor to work.

```typescript
providers: [
    { provide: HTTP_INTERCEPTORS,          ⟶   Interceptor service
     useClass: AuthInterceptor,            ⟶   Name of Interceptor class
        multi: true },
        ]
```

(App.module.ts)

```typescript
import { AuthInterceptor } from './auth.interceptor';
import { BrowserModule } from '@angular/platform-browser';
import { NgModule } from '@angular/core';

import { AppRoutingModule } from './app-routing.module';
import { AppComponent } from './app.component';
import { HttpClientModule, HTTP_INTERCEPTORS }
from '@angular/common/http';

@NgModule({
  declarations: [AppComponent, Child1Component],
  imports: [BrowserModule, AppRoutingModule, HttpClientModule],
  providers: [
    { provide: HTTP_INTERCEPTORS, useClass: AuthInterceptor, multi: tr
ue },
  ],
  bootstrap: [AppComponent],
})
export class AppModule {}
```

Libraries that needs to be imported are :-

```typescript
1.    import { HttpClientModule} from '@angular/common/http';
2.    import { HTTP_INTERCEPTORS } from '@angular/common/http';
```

Following is a basic example to get an understanding of interceptor :-

(app.component.ts)

```typescript
import { Component, OnInit } from '@angular/core';
import { HttpClient } from '@angular/common/http';

@Component({
  selector: 'app-root',
  templateUrl: './app.component.html',
  styleUrls: ['./app.component.css']
})
export class AppComponent implements OnInit {
  title = 'Interceptors Demo';
  constructor(private http: HttpClient) {}
```

```typescript
  ngOnInit(): void {}
  send(): void {
    this.http.get('http://localhost:51763/api/values').subscribe((res)
=> {
      alert('data: ' + res);
    });
  }
}
```

(app.component.html)

```html
<p>{{title}}</p>
<button (click)="send()">Send Request</button>
```

(auth.interceptor.ts)

```typescript
import { Injectable } from '@angular/core';
import {
  HttpRequest,
  HttpHandler,
  HttpEvent,
  HttpInterceptor,
} from '@angular/common/http';
import { Observable } from 'rxjs';

@Injectable()
export class AuthInterceptor implements HttpInterceptor {
  constructor() {}

  intercept(
    request: HttpRequest<unknown>,
    next: HttpHandler
  ): Observable<HttpEvent<unknown>> {
    alert('interceptor starts..');
    return next.handle(request);
  }
}
```

(app.module.ts)

```typescript
import { AuthInterceptor } from './auth.interceptor';
import { BrowserModule } from '@angular/platform-browser';
import { NgModule } from '@angular/core';

import { AppRoutingModule } from './app-routing.module';
import { AppComponent } from './app.component';
import { HttpClientModule, HTTP_INTERCEPTORS } from
'@angular/common/http';

@NgModule({
  declarations: [AppComponent, Child1Component],
  imports: [BrowserModule, AppRoutingModule, HttpClientModule],
  providers: [
    { provide: HTTP_INTERCEPTORS,
      useClass: AuthInterceptor,
      multi: true
    },
  ],
  bootstrap: [AppComponent],
})
export class AppModule {}
```

(Output) :-

Click the "Send Request" button, Interceptor will be activated before http request

After interceptor is activated, we will get our response from Api service

How to modify request object in interceptor ?

- **Immutable request** - We cannot directly modify a original request in Interceptor
- **Clone** - Need to Clone the request in order to modify it
- **Return modified request** - After modifying a request, we need to return a modified request instead of original request.

e.g.

```typescript
import { Injectable } from '@angular/core';
import {
  HttpRequest,
  HttpHandler,
  HttpEvent,
  HttpInterceptor,
} from '@angular/common/http';
import { Observable } from 'rxjs';

@Injectable()
export class AuthInterceptor implements HttpInterceptor {
  constructor() {}

  intercept(
    request: HttpRequest<unknown>,
    next: HttpHandler
  ): Observable<HttpEvent<unknown>> {

    const clonedRequest = request.clone({
      headers: request.headers.set('Authorization', 'Bearer ' + '1234')
    });
```

> We are cloning a request here because without cloning we cannot modify original request

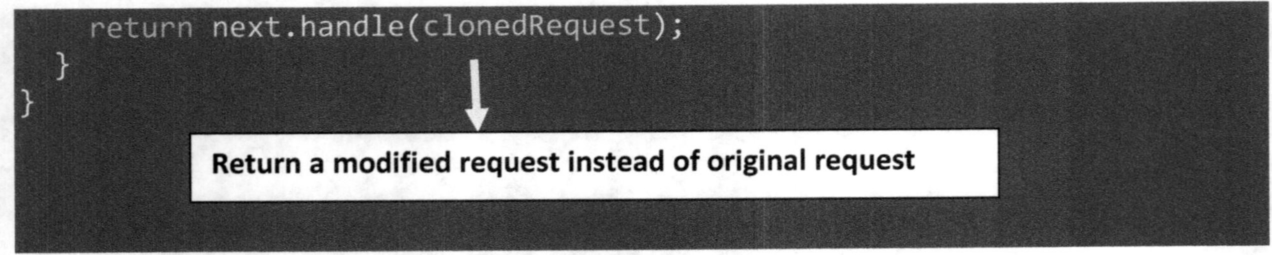

(Output) :-

Now, if you analyze a http request, then you can see the custom header that we have added in our interceptor

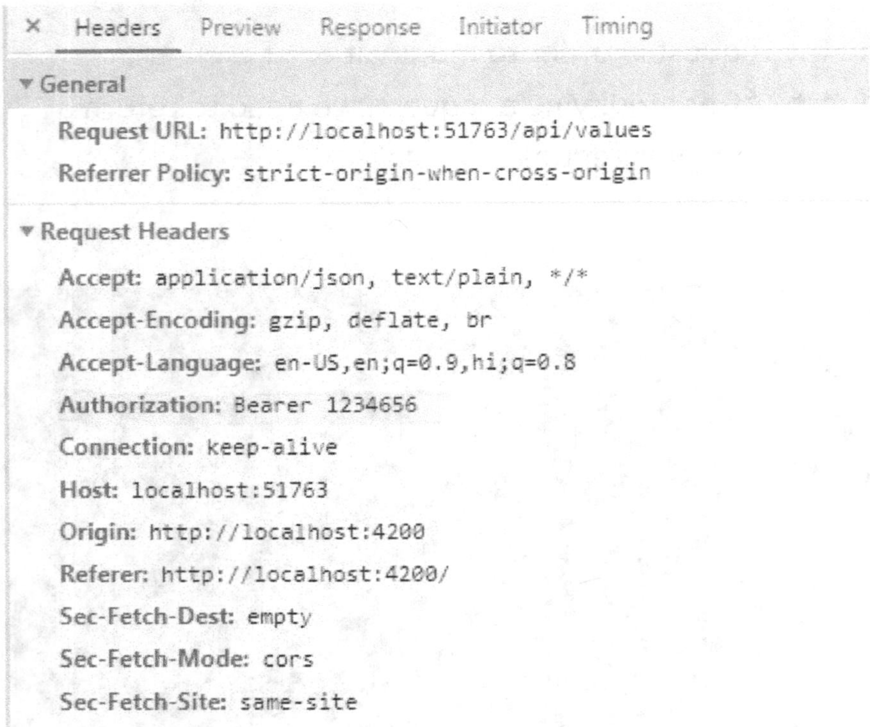

Using a interceptor , we can use token based authentication and can pass our tokens from interceptors.

How to handle response in interceptor ?

Interceptors always returns an observable which can be piped with operators like map, tap etc. to modify response

e.g.

```typescript
import { Injectable } from '@angular/core';
import { tap } from 'rxjs/operators';
import {
  HttpRequest,
  HttpHandler,
  HttpEvent,
  HttpInterceptor,
  HttpEventType,
} from '@angular/common/http';
import { Observable } from 'rxjs';

@Injectable()
export class AuthInterceptor implements HttpInterceptor {
  constructor() {}

  intercept(
    request: HttpRequest<unknown>,
    next: HttpHandler
  ): Observable<HttpEvent<unknown>> {
    const clonedRequest = request.clone({
    headers: request.headers.set('Authorization', 'Bearer ' + '1234')
    });
    return next.handle(clonedRequest).pipe(
      tap(
        (success) => {
          if (success.type === HttpEventType.Response) {
            alert('Interceptor response status : ' + success.status);
            alert('Interceptor response body : ' + success.body);
          }
        },
        (error) => {
          alert('Error: ' + error);
        }
      )
    );
  }
}
```

> We can pipe the observable with operators like tap if we don't want any modification in our response or map operator to modify response. We get access to properties of response like body, status etc.. only if HttpEventType.Response returns a true

(Output) :-

Now, we get access to response in Interceptor as well

localhost:4200 says

Interceptor response status : 200

OK

localhost:4200 says

Interceptor response body : value1,value2

OK

How to add multiple interceptors ?

- Multiple interceptors can also be added in a angular application.
- Like we can have authentication and logging interceptor in our application

e.g. :- In the following example we are adding 1 more interceptor in our
application (LogInterceptor). We need to add this interceptor in providers
array in AppModule

(app.module.ts)

```
import { LogInterceptor } from './log.interceptor';
import { AuthInterceptor } from './auth.interceptor';
import { BrowserModule } from '@angular/platform-browser';
import { NgModule } from '@angular/core';
```

```typescript
import { AppRoutingModule } from './app-routing.module';
import { AppComponent } from './app.component';
import { HttpClientModule, HTTP_INTERCEPTORS } from
 '@angular/common/http';

@NgModule({
  declarations: [AppComponent, Child1Component],
  imports: [BrowserModule, AppRoutingModule, HttpClientModule],
  providers: [
{ provide: HTTP_INTERCEPTORS, useClass: LogInterceptor, multi: true },
{ provide: HTTP_INTERCEPTORS, useClass: AuthInterceptor, multi: true }
  ],
  bootstrap: [AppComponent],
})
export class AppModule {}
```

Note :- **Ordering** is important here. The interceptors are executed in a order in which they are added in providers array.